RICHARD R. GAILLARDETZ

A Daring Promise

A SPIRITUALITY
OF CHRISTIAN MARRIAGE

A Crossroad Book
The Crossroad Publishing Company
New York

Acknowledgment is gratefully given to Riverhead Books, a division of Penguin Putnam, Inc., for permission to quote from *High Fidelity* by Nick Hornby, copyright © 1995 by Nick Hornby.

The Crossroad Publishing Company
481 Eighth Avenue, New York, NY 10001

Printed in the United States of America

Library of Congress Cataloging-in-Publication Data
Gaillardetz, Richard R., 1958-
     A daring promise : a spirituality of Christian marriage / Richard R.
Gaillardetz.
        p. cm.
     Includes bibliographical references.
     ISBN 0-8245-1935-3 (alk. paper)
        1. Marriage – Religious aspects – Catholic Church. 2. Catholic
Church – Doctrines.   I. Title.
BX2250 .G32 2002
248.4 – dc21
                                                                    2001005265

1   2   3   4   5   6   7   8   9   10   08   07   06   05   04   03   02

A Daring Promise

To Diana,
my true companion

Contents

Preface

I could barrage you with impressive citations of study after study, but it would be telling you what you already know — the institution of marriage is having a tough time of it these days. Not only is the frequency of divorce up, but results from the recent census confirm what many of us suspected: more and more people are avoiding marriage altogether. The likely causes are many, but I will leave that to the important work of social scientists and marriage therapists. What I hope to offer in this slim volume is the possibility that within the Christian tradition we can discover a faith-informed perspective that will not so much make marriage and family easier as it will explain why the hardness of it should not surprise us. It is hard precisely because, for the vast majority of Christians, marriage and family is the place where, by God's grace, we will work out our salvation.

I believe that the marital commitment that a man and a woman make to each other before God and in the midst of the Christian community is a most perilous undertaking, a journey fraught with risk. I am not speaking of the institution of marriage itself, nor am I speaking of the marital conventions that loosely come under the name "Christian," conventions that call for a "church wedding" presided over by a favorite minister. No, I mean the daring proposition that two people might unconditionally bind themselves together for life into an unknown future without destroying each other and/or their offspring in the process. To vow oneself to another before God is, I am convinced, one of the most radical things we do as Christians.

I am very much at home within my own Roman Catholic tradition. Still, I think that our tradition has been reluctant to explore the particular way in which the call to holiness that we all receive at our baptism is realized within the context of faithful married life. As Mary Anne McPherson Oliver has observed, a quick perusal of those who have been canonized by the Catholic Church, and thereby elevated as models of holiness, promises little insight into marital spirituality: "The only married saints canonized in the twentieth century have been martyrs or stigmatics, widow/foundresses of religious orders, and husbands who left wife and family to become missionaries or hermits."[1] This disparity says much about the gap between rhetoric and reality in Catholicism's position on marriage as a path to holiness.

Over a decade into this hazardous adventure, I have learned just enough to remain humbled by the mysterious reality of Christian marriage. What I do know is that my commitment to my wife, Diana, was and is the most significant single commitment I have made in my life. Writing about this commitment is itself somewhat perilous because I have by no means mastered the virtues that this commitment demands. This book might best be viewed not as a marriage manual in which the author unlocks the secrets of a successful marriage but rather something more akin to a pilgrim's journal in which I seek to record something of the spiritual topography of the marriage relationship. There is, of course, a difficulty with this approach, for the landscape that I know best is that which I have encountered in my own marriage. As lovely and beguiling and, yes, daunting as that particular countryside is, it belongs to my journey (or, to be more precise, our journey), and not that of any other. Yet I dare hope that in my reflections readers might find some insight to help them along their own marital pilgrimage. If by way of these pages they cultivate a heightened attentiveness to both the beautiful scenery and the rugged terrain married couples must negotiate along the way, I will judge this book a great success.

What follows is an exploration in marital spirituality. I do not pretend to offer a comprehensive sacramental theology of marriage. For that readers would do well to look to reliable works by Michael Lawler, Theodore Mackin, and others.[2] Rather, it is my desire to bring two different perspectives into conversation: (1) a theologically informed view of marriage that is faithful to the deep wisdom of our Christian tradition, and (2) an honest reading of the lived experience of marriage with all of its joys and struggles. An authentic spirituality of marriage will be effective to the extent that it emerges out of this kind of conversation.

The first chapter will lay a necessary foundation, beginning with some basic religious convictions that can ground Christian spirituality. Too much that passes for "spirituality" these days presents itself as an alternative to doctrine. Given the way in which Christian doctrine has so often been presented, this reaction is understandable. Still, a spirituality that truly merits being called Christian ought in some way to build upon basic Christian convictions.

In the second chapter I reflect on marriage as an invitation into the life of communion to which all of us are called. What is distinctive about marriage, I believe, is the public witness to this life of communion. To marry, at least from a Christian perspective, is to make our marital relationship, in a very concrete way, the concern of the church and a gift to the world. We commit ourselves to be a visible sign of what it means to live in communion with God and neighbor. Frightening though it may sound, we are called to become *martyres*, witnesses to a distinctive view of human life and fulfillment.

The third chapter turns to the way in which marriage stands, not only as an invitation to communion, but also as a summons to conversion; indeed, the marriage relationship becomes that privileged place wherein married couples work out their salvation. In marriage we enter into the dying and rising of Christ as we embrace our spouse as more than the source for the fulfillment of our needs and desires — our spouse is the mysterious "other" who cajoles and sometimes demands our growth.

The connection between marriage and salvation is important. In North America we encounter strong forces that would privatize religion. Yet for Christians salvation is never a private undertaking. We are creatures made for relationship, and our salvation can never be divorced from the web of relationships in which we live and realize our humanity. God's saving work is effected in and through our relationships with others. For those who submit to the saving pedagogy of marriage, the social context of salvation is felt all the more acutely. Marriage offers the opportunity to experience in a most intimate and sublime way comfort and solace in the arms of a spouse who commits himself or herself to us without condition. Perhaps less obvious to the nonmarried person, marriage also means submitting oneself to having another person "in your face" daily, confronting you with your own weaknesses, your private demons, and your need for conversion.

The fourth chapter turns to the question of marital sexuality and finds inspiration in a rereading of the familiar story of the creation of man and woman in the book of Genesis. There we discover that the heart of human sexuality lies in our capacity for vulnerability and transparency before another. The connections between marriage and sexuality are strong and complex. Here Christians are confronted with the ambiguity of our own religious tradition. It is a tradition that has affirmed the sacred and even sacramental significance of the marriage covenant even as it has been unable to purge a persistent suspicion about the intrinsic goodness of sexuality. Within Catholicism, the theological significance of conjugal relations has swung like a pendulum between two extremes. Great voices in our tradition have been all too willing to limit the goodness of marital sex to childbearing and being a "remedy to concupiscence." It should be remembered, however, that these perspectives, harsh and pessimistic by modern standards, often moderated far more extreme denunciations of sexuality. In the last fifty years, the pendulum has swung in the opposite direction. Catholic literature, including many official church documents, is quick to speak of the theological significance and beauty of marital sex, but in such highly romanticized language that many couples find little connection between this lofty prose and what they experience in their bedrooms.

In the fifth chapter I turn to the gift and challenge of parenthood within the marriage relationship. Most approaches to Christian marriage attend to the responsibilities that a parent has to the children. I am no parenting expert, and so the focus in this chapter will be not on parenting skills but rather on how the vocation to parent our children informs our own spiritual pilgrimage.

Though I take complete responsibility for what appears on these pages, there is a real sense in which my wife, Diana, is the co-author of this volume. While the words and overarching structure are mine, the wisdom, such as it is, is the shared fruit of a journey we have taken together as we have struggled to make our marriage "work." I am grateful that she has trusted me enough to allow our marriage to be "broken open" and mined for insight in these pages. Our four boys, David, Andrew, Brian, and Gregory, are now old enough to grasp something of what it means to say that "Dad is writing a book." Yet until sports heroes, astronauts, or wizards find their way onto these pages, my sons are likely to remain unimpressed. For this too I am grateful; they are often my surest anchor as I float adrift on a sea of theological musings.

I have been blessed along the way with many gracious and wise friends who have offered me so much. It is the sad lot of too many men in our culture to go through life accompanied only by "pals" with whom they can share a drink, watch a ball game, or play a round of golf, but with whom they do not feel comfortable engaging in what, for lack of another name, I will call "soul-talk." I have been extraordinarily fortunate to have male friends who have had the courage to speak with honesty and integrity about the graces and burdens of marriage and family: Rob Wething, Bob Cowgill, Richard Nimz, Wade Quinn, Tom Williams, Kevin O'Brien, and John Rooney. I am also grateful for the perceptive insight offered by women friends like Beth Nimz, Sandra Derby, Nancy Delavalle, and especially Mary Comeaux, who now, I am confident, holds us up in prayer as she abides in the communion of the blessed in heaven.

Diana and I have found solace and support in the wise and tender arms of a married couple, Winnie and Wally Honeywell, who have been wonderful mentors for us. Our own halting insights have often been confirmed, refined, and developed in their honest testimony. Our good fortune in being able to count them as friends and guides also serves as an admonishment to the church: we desperately need married mentors to help young couples stay the course.

I must also acknowledge those who graciously offered constructive commentary on early drafts of this work: Sidney Callahan, John Cockayne, Michael Downey, Fran Ferder, John Heagle, Winnie Honeywell, Nicki Maddox, John Rooney, and David Thomas. Finally I want to express my gratitude to the marketing and editorial team at Crossroad who have done so much to make the publishing process a pleasant and rewarding experience, particularly Gwendolin Herder, Paul McMahon, John Tintera, and John Eagleson.

Chapter One

The Shape of
Christian Spirituality

I recall the period early in our marriage when I was first confronted with the need for a marital spirituality. I was just completing my doctoral studies and had foolishly agreed to teach in a summer program at a university some four hundred miles away. Our twins were only two months old when we packed up all of the baby paraphernalia, clothes, books, and my computer, piled into our little Toyota, and headed off. We were housed in a dingy building that appeared as if it had once been an army barracks. Concrete floors, few windows, and broken-down furniture greeted us as we walked into our apartment. I was teaching all day and preparing for my dissertation defense in the evening. Diana was stuck in the apartment with twin infants and, with few exceptions, no friends or extended family to support her. I would leave at 7:30 a.m. to the sight of Diana sitting on the couch with both babies in her arms screaming. I would return home at 4:30 p.m. to the same sight, now accompanied by a glare from my wife that I best not describe. The evenings were spent in petty bickering as Diana pleaded for well-deserved "time off" while I complained about needing to prepare for my dissertation defense. The nights were an endless succession of interruptions as each baby needed to be fed or have a diaper changed at three-hour intervals. Neither of us slept more than four hours a night. Both resented the other if only because we dared not resent the children. Marital "intimacy" was the last thing on our minds as each of us fought off exhaustion. Somewhere during those four weeks the thought began to creep into each of our minds that getting married was a horrible mistake. This is not what we bargained for, what we stayed up until the late hours fantasizing about in the heady days of our engagement. There, little more than two years into our marriage, we found ourselves staring into the abyss.

I believe that many couples come to such a point in their relationship. It is the point when the relationship stops being effortless and becomes work, work that can feel exhausting and futile. We survived that summer, though to this day I am not sure how. There was no great epiphany or profound experience that constituted the clear turning point. Call it the grace of the sacrament if you like, all I know is that we began working harder to voice our resentments and frustrations directly to each other.

The image that comes to my mind for what began to happen in our relationship is drawn from a childhood memory of being on the stern of a large river boat, mesmerized by the soothing movement of the paddlewheel churning up the murky river water as it propelled the boat upstream. As we approached the dock the pilot shifted the engine into reverse. The paddlewheel's steady rhythm diminished, slowly coming to a stop, and then, after a discernible pause, the wheel only gradually and with the utmost of effort began to turn in the opposite direction. That summer saw a gradual but real reversal in the cycle of our own relations. The pattern of caustic complaints and sarcastic responses slowly gave way to a new pattern of care toward one another. The difficulties did not disappear, but each of us seemed to recognize, beyond our own pain and frustration, the effort our spouse was putting forth, and that mutual recognition triggered a reversal.

In retrospect, as I reflect on that difficult time, it is evident to me that the resources we drew upon constitute the foundations for what I have in mind by the term "spirituality." Without some authentic spirituality it is impossible for a marriage to survive such times and ultimately flourish. "Spirituality" is a relatively modern term. At one time it suggested a kind of piety, naming the concrete ways in which we incorporate prayer into our lives. Today it often refers to the "otherworldly," the mystical or paranormal. Some use the term in vague reference to the "depth" dimension of human existence. I will use the word "spirituality" to refer to the particular contour and texture of our encounter with God's saving grace in our daily lives. Any authentic spirituality, by revealing to us God's action in our lives, also discloses our truest identity; we "find" ourselves in our relationships with God and one another. A spirituality of marriage, then, will be concerned with the distinct manner in which God's transforming presence and action are encountered in our marriages. A marital spirituality should help us discover the ways in which, through our fidelity to the spiritual discipline of faithful marital living, we discover our truest identity before God.

There is a tendency here in the United States to distinguish between being spiritual and being religious. Many who consider themselves spiritual persons would not claim to be religious because they do not align themselves with any organized religious tradition. Yet spirituality need not be divorced from institutional religion. In fact, I believe that an authentic spirituality flourishes best when it draws from the resources of a larger religious tradition. There are several reasons for this.

First, a religious tradition offers us a "language of grace" by which we can name the experience of both God's call and our response. I recall a past experience in a twelve-step program of the kind associated with Alcoholics Anonymous. This program has helped millions of people recover from the hell of addiction and co-dependency. It engages the individual in a rigorous, yet undeniably spiritual process as the addict is invited to "surrender to a higher power." On a particular twelve-step retreat, I sat in a circle with others who spoke with such tremendous courage and honesty about their battles with their particular addictions and the ways in which God was assisting them in this battle. Many of these people belonged to my own tradition of Roman Catholicism and yet were seeking healing not from the ministry of the church but from this twelve-step community.

I was so saddened by the realization that as Roman Catholics, many who were there felt they could not turn to their own church for help; they dared not reveal their brokenness among other Catholics. I am convinced the problem is not unique to Catholicism. I recall a Protestant radio evangelist once commenting ruefully that the church is the only human institution that "kills its wounded." Far too many people, like the broken souls on this retreat, fear being judged, ostracized, or, perhaps worse, simply ignored by their church and so seek support elsewhere.

I felt a deep frustration on that retreat. The twelve-step program presented a spirituality grounded in "surrender to a higher power," and it offered the "Big Book" as a collection of often inspiring stories and aphorisms. Yet in general it lacked the rich spiritual resources, the language of grace, that could be found in the Christian tradition to help the broken deal with their situation. I was saddened at the realization that for these men, my church, in possession of this marvelous heritage of spirituality, was not experienced as a community that welcomed and accepted them in their brokenness. Its rich lexicon of grace was inaccessible to them. One of the most pressing pastoral imperatives in the church today is to heal this breach between the human longing for an authentic spirituality and the distrust of institutional religion.

The second reason for developing a spirituality within a specific religious tradition is that each tradition offers us foundational stories, rituals, and doctrines that help give substance and shape to the spiritual life. How did we ever get to this place where the particulars of our belief have come to be seen as irrelevant to our spirituality? The tendency is to blame this on the rise of both individualism and religious relativism in our time. While these influences are real, some of the blame must be placed at the feet of the churches themselves. The Christian churches have often failed to make the case that particular Christian beliefs are relevant. Our most basic doctrinal commitments have been tainted by polemics (e.g., Catholics against Protestants), overlaid with speculative interpretations, and articulated in such arcane language that they cease to move us.

Many people who might be interested in belonging to a particular church become "turned off" by traditional treatments of Christian doctrine. For many who consider themselves active Christians the question is not so much whether they "believe in" traditional doctrines like the Trinity or the Incarnation, but whether they can make a real connection between these formal beliefs and what concerns them in their daily life. Consequently, one challenge for contemporary spirituality is to lay open the profound connections between the substance of our daily lives and the wisdom of our most basic doctrinal commitments.

The third reason for exploring spirituality within a larger religious tradition is that the stories, rituals, and doctrines of a particular tradition can serve as a vital corrective to the human tendency to fashion a spirituality that merely confirms our more superficial wants and desires. Many accuse contemporary New Age spirituality of neopaganism or gnosticism, accusations that strike me as rather simplistic. I believe the most serious failing of New Age spirituality lies in its studied eclecticism, the way in which individual seekers are encouraged to draw certain beliefs and practices from various religious traditions in accord with their own particular needs. There is no prophetic dimension, no larger tradition that can go beyond merely meeting people's spiritual needs to call them to growth and conversion.

What we believe and *how* we believe are equally important. My particular faith convictions should play a vital role in my spiritual life. The distinctive doctrinal commitments of my faith are what give shape to my spirituality. And to the extent that my marriage is truly a Christian marriage, these beliefs must also shape my experience of marriage. In the background reading I did in preparation for this volume, I was impressed with the way authors who wrote on the spirituality of marriage so gracefully and effectively wove the insights of contemporary psychology and family systems theory into their reflections. This approach has been of enormous help for many married couples who have looked to these books for concrete guidance in their married life. However, I was somewhat less impressed with the attempts to integrate basic Christian doctrinal commitments into marital spirituality. The

implicit assumption seemed to be that such a doctrinal inte-
gration was more appropriate to a systematic or sacramental
theology of marriage than to marital spirituality.

Throughout this book, as I reflect on marital spirituality,
I will be drawing on four basic doctrinal commitments that I
believe have much to contribute to a spirituality of marriage:
(1) at the core of our humanity is the experience of desire,
an inner drive for communion with God and one another;
(2) the incarnation reveals to us the fulfillment of that desire and of our very humanity in the person of Jesus Christ;
(3) the suffering, death, and resurrection of Jesus, often called
the "paschal mystery," offers us the way of salvation and the
paradoxical logic of authentic human fulfillment; (4) the true
wisdom of the Christian doctrine of the Trinity is that God *is*
communion and therefore is discovered whenever and wherever we give ourselves over to the life of communion. These
doctrinal commitments may seem very formal and abstract,
but I believe that they are vital for developing an authentic
marital spirituality. Let me offer an initial exploration of each
of these convictions as a foundation for later reflection on
marital spirituality.

We Are Made for God

I have a good friend who experienced a difficult bout with
depression over a period of several months. She shared with
me that there were times when she found it difficult just to
get out of bed in the morning. Yet she did, if only because
she knew that getting out of bed in the morning is what we
do when we are healthy, and though she knew she was not
healthy, she felt that the only thing that prevented her from
taking her own life was acting as if she were.

Why do healthy people get out of bed each morning and face the world? There are certainly days when it involves little more than habit, but I believe there is something more. I believe that at some deep center of our being we expect something from the day or, at the very least, we long for something from the day. Within each of us there is an inner restlessness, an insufficiency that impels us to engage our world, to forge meaningful relationships with others, to exercise our imaginations. The vitality of a human life can be measured by the intensity of one's desire. We know we are truly alive when we experience a drive for the "more" of life. I do not mean by this that false desire, the consumerist impulse, forged by modern marketing strategies. There desire does not emerge from the spiritual wellspring within but is crassly manufactured and manipulated by companies eager to convince us that product X will finally sate that longing artificially planted within us. The expression of authentic human desire lies not in a desire for "things"; it is a much deeper impulse for human fulfillment.

Human desire is the source of our spiritual energy. It is what impels us in our most creative labors and moves us to enter into relationship with others. It is encountered when a man aches for the woman he loves, when a software designer pushes himself to perfect a product he is creating, when a mother longs for an absent child, when a lawyer defends the defenseless in a search for justice, when a bereaved soul yearns to have others know her pain and loss.

It is bedrock biblical wisdom that the human person was not created for isolation; the way of the hermit has always been the cautious exception rather than the rule in the Christian tradition. No, we are made for communion, driven into relationship by a deep sense that by connecting with another we might find wholeness and be sated. For a time we may even experience something of this wholeness. But it does not, and indeed cannot, last. The desires that well up within us cannot be definitively satisfied by anything in our world. In a well-known passage, St. Augustine wrote in his *Confessions,* "Our hearts are restless, Lord, until they rest in you."[3] Perhaps no Christian writer so perceptively grasped the spiritual power of desire as the twelfth-century Cistercian monk Bernard of Clairveaux. For Bernard, "desire is the form love takes in our earthly existence."[4] This sense of human longing for relationship is not rooted in some animal need for mating and the survival of the species. Bernard believed that the source of human desire was the image and likeness of God inscribed in our very being. The longing for the communion we experience with another wells up from our longing for God and offers us a real yet imperfect participation in the one divine communion that alone can completely fulfill us.

Human desire, quite obviously, is important for an understanding of marriage. After all, without the desire to love and be loved by another, no one would ever enter into a relationship as demanding as marriage. This is why marriages are most at risk during those periods when one or another of the spouses experiences a waning of desire. I am not primarily speaking of sexual desire but of that basic desire for communion with another and the way of life that real communion offers. Any authentic marital spirituality must attend to this basic human experience of desire and the drive for communion with another.

Jesus Reveals to Us Our Humanity

At the Second Vatican Council the bishops offered a wonderful agenda for renewing the Catholic Church. One of their

most remarkable documents was entitled the Pastoral Constitution on the Church in the Modern World, *Gaudium et spes*.
In this document they called the church to look at the world
not just as an enemy to be conquered but as a dialogue partner. The church must try to understand the problems and
challenges faced by humanity today out of the conviction
that Christianity can offer a meaningful response. Christianity
offers the world Jesus Christ, not as some otherworldly inter-
mediary foreign to human experience, but as the fulfillment
of all we were created to be:

> In reality it is only in the mystery of the Word made flesh
> that the mystery of humanity truly becomes clear....
> Christ the new Adam, in the very revelation of the mys-
> tery of the Father and of his love, fully reveals humanity
> to itself and brings to light its very high calling.[5]

We refer to this as the mystery of the incarnation, the belief that in Jesus of Nazareth God is encountered not simply
through imperfect intermediaries but in an unprecedented
immediacy. In Jesus, God has definitively taken our human
reality as God's own. Jesus is the human face of God's love
for us.

And yet our sense of Jesus has been distorted by the fact
that the four gospels in the New Testament do not offer de-
tailed biographies of Jesus' life but theologically interpreted,
selective accounts of, for the most part, only his public ministry. Consequently, when we think of Jesus we recall dynamic
preaching and spellbinding stories, walking on water, changing water into wine, raising Lazarus from the dead, healing
the blind and the lame, and exorcising demons. He is for us
the Son of God whom we worship. This reflects the kind of
encounter with Jesus that moved Peter, James, and John to fall

down on their knees at Jesus' transfiguration. However, it is difficult for us to find anything of *ourselves* in this view of Jesus. This brings us to an often overlooked question. The Bible reports to us the dramatic circumstances surrounding Jesus' birth, the many signs and wonders that Jesus performed much later in life, the great teachings he left us, and the redemptive power of his suffering, death, and resurrection. But what of the thirty or so years of Jesus' life between his birth and his public ministry? We know scarce little of the life of Jesus during this time, but we can surmise a few likely facts. First, Jesus was a layperson. It may seem odd to put the matter that way but it is an important point. The tendency to think of Jesus in priestly terms has been no doubt encouraged by the subsequent Catholic theological and sacramental tradition that spoke of the ordained priest of the church acting as "another Christ" or functioning "in the person of Christ the head of the church." Yet there is no biblical evidence that Jesus was of either Levitical or priestly descent. Even in his public ministry he acted always as a Jewish layperson. There is but one book of the New Testament, the Letter to the Hebrews, that refers to Jesus as our high priest. Nowhere else in the New Testament is priestly language ever applied to Jesus. If Jesus was a Jewish layman, then he could not rely on any official authority — his authority was an authority of character not of office. This means that at least prior to his public ministry, since he was not born into a priestly tribe his life would not have been any different from any other Jewish male.

And what of Jesus' marital status? The New Testament is completely silent on this matter. However, in light of the frequent mention of other key figures having wives or having left their wives to follow Jesus, it is unlikely that a wife of Jesus would go without note. But what can we infer from this? The fact that Jesus was probably not married itself tells us little. Apart from one brief passage that speaks of those who make themselves eunuchs for the kingdom of God (Matt. 19:12) there is little to suggest what, if any, religious significance there may have been to Jesus' celibacy. It was very common for women to marry young, often in their early teens. But this was not necessarily the case for men who frequently married much later in life.

Being single is one thing, being a consecrated celibate — choosing lifelong celibacy as an expression of one's religious commitment — is something else altogether. Even if Jesus never married, there is little evidence that he considered himself a formal, consecrated celibate (in the tradition, for example, of the Jewish Essene community, which set celibacy as a precondition for membership in their monastic community), at least prior to his public ministry. While the matter cannot be pursued here, this simple fact about Jesus might yield great fruit for a spirituality of the single person. It suggests that in Jesus we discover a person who was neither married nor a consecrated celibate and yet found human fulfillment in free and intimate relationships with friends of both sexes.

Mark 6:3 tells us that he was a woodworker, that is, a basic craftsman who would have built rudimentary furniture, plows, or yokes. As such he would have been a step or two above a slave or day laborer in socioeconomic class.[6] In any event, we know that Jesus practiced a trade. We have no record of his performing great miracles during this time. There is no indication of any adolescent "sermons on the mount" save for Luke's account of unlikely historicity relating a brief foray in the temple at the age of twelve.

We do know that aside from his practicing a trade, Jesus presumably took care of a family. Indirect biblical evidence leads us to conclude that Joseph had died long before Jesus began his public ministry. The frequent references to Mary and his "brothers and sisters"[7] suggest that whatever precise relations bound him to these "brothers and sisters" they saw themselves as "family" who felt that it was within their rights to lay claim to his attention (see Mark 3:31–35). To put the matter straightforwardly, by all appearances Jesus lived a fairly ordinary and unexceptional life prior to his brief public ministry. He practiced a trade and attended to his family obligations to his mother and other kin. What is the significance of this? It suggests that when God chose to embrace humanity in this unique fashion almost two thousand years ago, he embraced *our* world, a world filled with mundane daily tasks for which few are canonized: the world of family and work, the world of simple meals, simple homes, and simple pleasures. He took all that is ordinary and, to our modern eyes, boring and without value, and he blessed it, manifesting thereby its holiness.

Our belief in the incarnation is, among other things, a belief in the intrinsic sacredness of the most basic of human activities and relationships: work, leisure, and family. A spirituality of marriage will need to find God not only in church or on one's knees in prayer, but in shared labor, in shared leisure, and in the characteristic practices and commitments necessary for nurturing a shared household.

The Paschal Mystery as the Paradoxical Logic of Human Fulfillment

For many Christians, belief in the saving work of Christ begins and ends with the passion, death, resurrection, and ascension of Christ, sometimes called the "paschal mystery." The term "paschal" recalls the Hebrew Passover (Pasch), in which God delivered the Israelites from slavery into freedom. Christians hold that in death Christ too "passed over" into the Father, effecting our own liberation from sin. Many Christian traditions hold that the celebration of the sacraments, particularly through baptism and the eucharist, is a means of ritually uniting ourselves with Christ in this paschal mystery. But it is a mistake to think of the paschal mystery only in connection with the final events of Jesus' life. For what transpired in the last days of Jesus' life on earth was but a dramatic manifestation of a pattern of life, an interior movement, that characterized all of Jesus' life. He always acted in perfect accord with an interior spiritual rhythm that we might characterize simply as life-death-life. The central challenge of Christian life is to internalize and make this spiritual rhythm our own. With Jesus we are to *live* out of the assurance that we are God's good creatures, *die* to any tendency to make ourselves the ultimate reality in the universe, and *live* anew in lives of loving attentiveness and service to others. What Jesus lived, he also taught: "Unless a grain of wheat falls into the ground and dies, it remains only a single grain; but if it dies it yields a rich harvest" (John 12:24). In his life and in his teaching he offered us a new vision of human wholeness in which "death" and "life" are infused with new meaning. In this vein Ronald Rolheiser distinguishes between two kinds of death and two kinds of life:

> First, regarding two kinds of death: there is *terminal* death and there is *paschal* death. Terminal death is a death that ends life and ends possibilities. Paschal death, like terminal death, is real. However, paschal death is a death that, while ending one kind of life, opens the per-

son undergoing it to receive a deeper and richer form of life. The image of the grain of wheat falling into the ground and dying so as to produce new life is an image of paschal death. There are also two kinds of life: there is *resuscitated* life and there is *resurrected* life. Resuscitated life is when one is restored to one's former life and health, as is the case with someone who has been clinically dead and is brought back to life. Resurrected life is not this. It is not a restoration of one's old life but the reception of a radically new life.[8]

We are thus introduced to the peculiar program for Christian living. If you want to be happy, seek the happiness of others. If you would be fulfilled, abandon the quest for fulfillment. To delight in the gifts of creation you must learn on occasion to abstain from them. To know the joy of the feast you must embrace the longing that arises from the fast.

For the martyrs of the early church, their witness to the power of the paschal mystery took the most dramatic form imaginable: it was through the free offering of their very lives that they gave eloquent and sometimes shocking testimony to the power of the cross and resurrection. The witness of the early martyrs eventually gave way to the asceticism of monastic and consecrated religious life. Those who publicly committed themselves to poverty, chastity, obedience, and sometimes stability (the commitment to live the balance of one's life in one religious house), were freely embracing the limits these vows imposed upon them in order to more profoundly enter into the paschal pattern of life-death-life. The church still benefits greatly from the evangelical witness of consecrated religious who embrace the paschal mystery in such a public way through their vows. Yet the time has come to acknowledge that the way of Christian asceticism so often associated with "the vowed life" is not limited to consecrated religious men and women. Authentic Christian marriage is also a form of public "vowed life."

The sacrament of marriage has from the very beginning of Christianity been shrouded in ambiguity and suspicion. It was not universally recognized as a sacrament until the thirteenth century. Significant disagreements over when a marriage was considered indissoluble and other such questions obscured its evangelical value. In marriage, two people exchange vows, freely entering into a permanent covenantal relationship with one another. As with consecrated religious life, the heart of this commitment, its spiritual core, is the freely accepted decision to embrace the limits that these vows impose. This means that marriage is every bit as much a paschal or ascetical vocation as that of the monk, vowed religious, nun, or priest. As we shall see in the next two chapters, marriage too involves the free embrace of limits as an opportunity to enter into the paschal mystery.

The book of Genesis reminds us that we are created in the image and likeness of God (Gen. 1:26–27). It is a way of saying that there is something vital within us that allows us to share or participate in God's life. When we are authentically human and give ourselves over to our deepest longing for human communion we are, at the same time, participating in the divine. This idea of participation in the life of God has been affirmed in many different ways by some of the greatest voices in the Christian tradition. Yet its implications for spirituality have often been overlooked. To understand it we must turn to one of the most fundamental and yet misunderstood doctrines in our tradition, the Trinity.

The Trinity

Most Christians believe in the doctrine of the Trinity, that basic Christian teaching that God exists as three divine persons sharing in one divine nature. Yet because, on the face of it, this claim makes no sense (how can $3=1$?) their belief fails to challenge the conventional ways in which they imagine God.

What is this conventional way of imagining God? Most of us think of God as an individual super-being. As such, we believe that God is infinitely more powerful than ourselves, all-knowing, all-loving, but just another being nonetheless. We will use Trinitarian language, Father, Son, and Spirit, but in ways that suggest God is, if not a divine individual, a kind of divine consortium — two men and a bird, as some have put it. Both viewpoints actually cash out in much the same way. Whether God is conceived as a single super-being whose existence adds to the total entities that exist in our universe, or as a divine consortium — in either case God will be another individual being or set of beings to whom I must relate alongside the other claims on my attention.

This way of imagining God has had a pervasive and almost completely negative impact on Christian spirituality because it places God in competition with my other, more worldly concerns. My whole life will then be an endless tug-of-war between the matters that demand my attention in the daily course of human affairs — preparing classes, buying groceries, playing with my children, talking with my wife — and my religious obligations to God. Years ago the great Jesuit scientist and mystic Teilhard de Chardin captured the consequences of such a way of imagining God:

> I do not think I am exaggerating when I say that nine out of ten practicing Christians feel that [human] work is

always at the level of a "spiritual encumbrance." In spite
of the practice of right intentions, and the day offered
every morning to God, the general run of the faithful
dimly feel that time spent at the office or the studio,
in the fields or in the factory, is time taken away from
prayer and adoration. It is impossible not to work —
that is taken for granted. Then it is impossible, too, to
aim at the deep religious life reserved for those who
have the leisure to pray or preach all day long. A few
moments of the day can be salvaged for God, yes, but
the best hours are absorbed, or at any rate, cheapened,
by material cares. Under the sway of this feeling, large
numbers of Catholics lead a double or crippled life in
practice.[9]

Such a perspective cannot help but have an impact on our
view of the Christian vocation to marriage and family. My
commitment to my spouse and children, as well as to my career, becomes a distraction that immediately relegates me to
second-class citizenship in the kingdom of God. Here the best
that a spirituality of marriage can offer is a way to "sacralize"
our marriage by desperately inserting as many religious moments into our day — snatches of time for scripture reading
or private devotions, early morning daily mass, grace at meals
and so on — that become our only hope for preserving some
frail contact with a God to whom we do not have the luxury
of "praying without ceasing."

Regrettably, in the Catholic tradition there are distorted
theologies of celibacy that assume this perspective and consequently suggest that the committed celibate, free from the
"distractions" of marriage and family, is better able to love
God.[10] From this came a spirituality of "detachment" in which

it was thought that spiritual growth meant detaching one-self from anything that distracted from God. When the great Trappist monk and spiritual writer Thomas Merton wrote of the spirituality of detachment, he felt compelled to clarify that detachment did not mean a detachment from things in themselves:

> Detachment from things does not mean setting up a contradiction between "things" and "God" as if God were another "thing" and as if His creatures were His rivals. We do not detach ourselves from things in order to attach ourselves to God, but rather we become detached *from ourselves* in order to see and use all things in and for God. This is an entirely new perspective which many sincerely moral and ascetic minds fail utterly to see. There is no evil in anything created by God, nor can anything of His become an obstacle to our union with Him. The obstacle is in our "self," that is to say in the tenacious need to maintain our separate, external, egotistical will.[11]

Were this image of God as a remote super-being our only available way of imaging God, there would not be any point in exploring a spirituality of marriage; the only realistic approach to marital spirituality within this framework would be the simple injunction: pray more! To counter this all too common imaginative framework we must recover the deeper insights from our Christian tradition embedded in the doctrine of the Trinity.

Our belief that God is triune means that God is *not* to be conceived as an individual super-being or set of "persons" that exists alongside all other beings in the cosmos. Rather the doctrine of the Trinity teaches us that God is best conceived as the divine source and superabundant dynamism of love, not an individual but a divine movement, not an object but the very spiritual atmosphere of our lives. In the early church the formal doctrinal language of the Trinity emerged out of a basic experience of God. Early Christians experienced Jesus as the concrete expression of God's love, and the Holy Spirit as both the divine atmosphere in which they encountered Christ and the divine power by which they were brought into communion with God in union with Christ.

Emerging Trinitarian doctrine named the *shape* of the Christian encounter with God. God was not a distant entity sending divine intermediaries. Rather, Christians experienced God as the divine source and superabundance of love being poured forth in Jesus of Nazareth, made effective by the Holy Spirit, and at every moment inviting the believer into transformative relationship. Conceiving the triune life of God as a divine movement toward us in love points toward the essential insight of Trinitarian doctrine, namely, that God's very being, what it is for God to be, is loving, life-giving relationship. God does not just *have* a love relationship with us, God *is* loving relationship. This means that an imaginative view of God's relationship to us must resist positing God as an individual being whose grace must be imported into our world. God is that holy mystery that bears the world up in its very existence. God is "Being-as-Communion."[12] There is no self-contained, divine individual residing in heaven far away from us; there is simply a dynamic movement of love that *is* God, "in whom we live and move and have our being." This imaginative framework also has strong biblical roots. St. Paul writes:

> God's love has been poured into our hearts through the
> Holy Spirit that has been given to us. For while we were

> still weak, at the right time Christ died for the ungodly. Indeed, rarely will anyone die for a righteous person — though perhaps for a good person someone might actually dare to die. But God proves his love for us in that while we still were sinners Christ died for us. (Rom. 5:5–8)

The Johannine literature also presents God not as an individual being whose many attributes (e.g., kindness, mercy, generosity) include "loving," but as love abiding:

> Beloved, let us love one another, because love is from God; everyone who loves is born of God and knows God. Whoever does not love does not know God, for God is love.... No one has ever seen God; if we love one another, God lives in us, and his love is perfected in us.... God is love, and those who abide in love abide in God, and God abides in them.... Those who say, "I love God," and hate their brothers or sisters, are liars; for those who do not love a brother or sister whom they have seen, cannot love God whom they have not seen. The commandment we have from him is this: those who love God must love their brothers and sisters also. (1 John 4:7–8, 12, 16, 20–21)

What we have is a biblical tradition alive to the way in which love does not just describe an attribute of God but names the essential *way* in which God is God. This view of God as fundamentally relational and engaged in our world has been expressed in the insights of the many giants of our tradition. St. Augustine captured something of it when he spoke of God as "closer to us than we are to ourselves." St. Thomas Aquinas assumed this perspective in his presentation of Creation,

not as an event in the distant past but as the ongoing relationship God has with the world. God is Creator because,
even now, God is sustaining all that is, bearing the world up
in divine love.

As Christianity developed a more precise Trinitarian language, it came to describe the shape of God's dynamic
movement toward us in the language of God, Word, and Spirit
or, alternatively, Father, Son, and Spirit. These terms should
not be construed, however, as the proper names of God. God
cannot be named in the sense that a name explains someone or something. Recall God's refusal to reveal to Moses the
divine name. Unlike the other gods of antiquity, Israel's God
was utterly sovereign, not to be manipulated by the controlling
power of "naming." This God is disclosed to Israel in divine
action, covenantal love. As Christians we should not imagine
that God has given to us what God withheld from Moses. God
is the mysterious "more" ever beyond us, yet always abiding
with us. God discloses God's self as holy mystery, not a riddle
to be solved but an inexhaustible source and realization of
love to be embraced.

The God of the covenant, the God of superabundant love
eternally "speaks," or expresses, divine love as Word and
makes that Word fertile and effective by the power of the
Spirit. The Trinity outlines the shape of this eternal divine
"speaking." It may be helpful to consider the root meaning
of the Hebrew word for "spirit," *ruah*, which literally means
"breath." When I speak a word to another, I attempt to communicate something of myself to that person. Yet that spoken
word is conveyed to the other by means of my breath. Of
course the recipient of my word does not focus on my breath
but rather on the word my breath vocalizes. In like manner
we might say that in God (the Father) love is uttered as an

eternal Word (the Son) and born by the holy breath of God (the Holy Spirit) we call Spirit. As triune, God who is love eternally offers God's self as love spoken and love made effective. Michael Downey describes the felt experience of this profound Christian conviction regarding the nature of God:

> While the teaching about the Trinity...may be dismissed as a vexing puzzle by many, in the ordinary lives of the Christian faithful there is indeed some grasp of the mystery which the doctrine seeks to express. In other words, there is often a deep experience of the Father as the originator and Pure Source of Love, Jesus Christ the Son who is that Love seen and heard in Word, and the Spirit as the ongoing and inexhaustible activity of that Love, drawing everything and everyone back to the origin and end of Love in the bonding of Love itself.[13]

The deep wisdom of Christian intuitions about the being of God lies in the Trinitarian affirmation that God is not a self-contained, distant, introverted God, but dynamic, personal, relational, fecund, and inclusive of all reality.

The spiritual challenge of our lives lies not in desperately setting aside moments for God alongside the other activities and commitments of our lives, but rather that of discovering in our basic human activities and commitments the possibility for communion with God *in* our communion with others. If God is love, if God is gift given eternally, then our participation in the life of God happens not by escaping our everyday world, but by entering more deeply into the life of love and that paradoxical logic of gift in which we receive most richly only when we make "gifting" others a way of life. In conventional Christian piety, prayer names "religious" moments and actions in our lives. The task of the spiritual life was to accumulate as many of these as possible. The perspective I am offering here is one in which prayer names those moments and activities when we consciously cultivate an awareness of the God who abides with us throughout the day. As for Christian marriage, it will offer us true communion with God when, and only when, our spousal relations are drawn into the pattern of divine love and the logic of divine gift revealed to us in Trinitarian doctrine.

These four doctrinal commitments provide a helpful foundation for exploring the spiritual dimension of married life. They place the marriage relationship within the context of the larger movement toward divine communion for which we were made as humans. We will have occasion to return to these basic convictions in the chapters ahead.

Questions for Reflection and Discussion

1. Do your consider yourself a "spiritual" person? Do you consider yourself a "religious" person? How do you make the connection between being religious and being spiritual in your own life?

2. Does reflection on the "hidden years" of Jesus, that time when he practiced a trade and took care of a family, have any impact on the way you think of your own daily responsibilities?

3. How does your own understanding of prayer relate to the two approaches discussed in this chapter: (1) prayer as a means of injecting "religious" moments into your daily life, or (2) prayer as the cultivation of a sense of God's abiding presence in your daily life?

Chapter Two

Marriage and the Life of Communion

I must confess to dreading occasions, at Christian weddings, in marriage preparation programs, or marriage enrichment retreats, at which I must hear someone address the spiritual significance of marriage. With notable exceptions these presentations too often either are insipid or offer an unrealistic vision of married life. When priests are offering these reflections, the generally poor quality might be due to the fact that many of them, lacking personal experience of married life, draw their reflections from either the notes they took in seminary courses or their own fantasies regarding what it was that they "gave up" in choosing celibacy. Of course this is not always the case. I do know many priests with a real respect for and considerable insight into marriage. They have learned much from the lived experience of the many engaged and married couples to whom they have ministered. Besides, some of the corniest things I have heard about marriage have often been uttered by married people who, frankly, ought to know better.

Is there a shared assumption that lies at the heart of these flawed reflections? I think so. Too often, accounts of marital spirituality present God as the transcendent "third party" in the marriage relationship. This perspective is depicted in the famous marriage emblem with three interlocking circles. In a similar vein one will hear of the importance of making "Christ the center of your marriage." This is usually followed by an admonition to couples to make shared prayer the foundation of their marriage. What could possibly be objectionable in this perspective? you ask. Does not Christian marriage presuppose the centrality of God in the couple's relationship? To justify my dissatisfaction with this approach to marital spirituality, let me begin with something of a personal confession.

Diana and I have never succeeded in sustaining a regular pattern of joint prayer in our marriage. This struggle is not uncommon for couples with children who must regularly fight to find time to be alone together. But that does not explain the matter entirely. I suspect that our difficulties praying together stem from our significantly different approaches to prayer. My wife is a convert to Catholicism and was raised with a spontaneous and improvisational style of prayer quite different from my own background in which prayer meant "saying prayers." These different styles are evident even in the ways we pray with our children. I am more inclined to introduce our children to the traditional prayers with which I was raised, while she is more likely to pray with them spontaneously or to lead our family in ad hoc prayer services at key family celebrations.

Over the years of our married life, our approaches to prayer have certainly changed. Diana has moved to a more contemplative style of prayer while my own prayer has been shaped more and more by the liturgy of the church. We are both, I believe, people of prayer, but we have yet to find a common style of prayer that is equally fulfilling. Our situation is certainly not going to fit the experience of every married couple. I know of several couples who have found ways to make common prayer the centerpiece of their marriage. I am reluctant to grant, however, that the spirituality of a marriage must be measured by the quality and frequency of the shared prayer of the couple. This is because, shocking as it may sound, I do not believe that God is a third party in our marriage. As I suggested in the last chapter, this viewpoint tends to imagine God as another being, a super-being to be sure, but nevertheless another individual being who must compete for our attention. I am convinced that the God of the Christian faith is not an individual super-being. Our God is not an individual anything but the very ground and source of our existence who sustains us and abides in us when we engage in what I have called the life of communion.

Prayer is by no means unimportant, be it individual prayer, shared prayer, or liturgical prayer. Yet conscious formal prayer is never a matter of invoking an absent God to become present but rather the cultivation of our awareness of the God who already abides in us as we give ourselves over to others. Whether couples cultivate this awareness together in joint prayer experiences, in their own moments of solitude, or in the celebration of the liturgy of the church, what is important is that they find ways to affirm and sustain their awareness of God's abiding presence as they live the life of communion.

The Life of Communion

If one of the cornerstones of Christian spirituality is the call to the life of communion, then marriage offers us one of the most vital ways of cultivating this life of communion. When a husband and wife attend to one another, not as objects for their own gratification but as subjects of infinite dignity and worth, they enter into the life of love and their communion with one another is, at the same time, communion with God.

This insight is, in my view, the indispensable foundation of any marital spirituality. God is found in the "between" of the relationship of husband and wife. In the book of Genesis we are told that we "are created in the image of God, male and female" (Gen. 1:27). The Orthodox bishop and theologian Kallistos Ware suggests boldly that in this biblical passage

> the image of God is given, not to the man alone or to the woman alone, but to the two of them together.... It comes to its fulfillment only in the "between" that unites them to each other. Personhood is a mutual gift; there is no true human unless there are at least two humans in communion with each other. To say "I am made in God's image" is to affirm: "I need you in order to be myself." The divine image is in this way a "relational" image, manifested not in isolation but in community — and, above all, in the primordial bond between husband and wife that is the foundation of all other forms of social life.[14]

To be human is to need relationship with another in order to "be myself." Marriage is simply a dramatic testimony to this basic human truth. In marriage we experience communion with our spouses not because we are each half-selves looking for a mate as our completion, but because in marriage we find ourselves in giving ourselves to another. This "shared life of communion" is a kind of theological shorthand for the diverse ways in which married couples, in the authenticity of their daily life together, abide in God *as they attend to one another in love.* I am suggesting here that God is not a third party who must regularly be called into the marriage relationship; God abides *in* the marriage relationship itself. In other words, sometimes our most profound experience of God comes, not when we are consciously focusing on God as in times of prayer and worship, but when we lovingly turn to embrace another in love. It follows then that the cultivation of an authentic marital spirituality will mean, not just more prayer, but the fostering of marital communion. Let us consider three concrete dimensions of this experience of marital communion: mutuality, intimacy, and companionship.

Mutuality

One often hears the word "mutuality" used in relation to marital life, but what does it really mean? Mutuality is manifested in human relationships wherever and whenever both parties recognize and acknowledge the giftedness of the other. This is quite different from the important, yet in itself insufficient, assertion that each spouse be treated as an equal. When we cultivate mutuality in our marriage we are learning to affirm not only the equality of each partner but also each one's unique giftedness.

Some of the most important work that must take place in a marriage relationship concerns the cultivation of mutuality. A few weeks ago my wife and I were able to get out for a rare "dinner date" without the kids. Most of the dinner conversations we have when we are alone together end up revolving around very practical questions, our calendars, our jobs, or concerns we have about one of our children. On this particular evening, however, we made a conscious decision to dedicate our dinner conversation exclusively to our marriage relationship. We decided to tell each other all of the ways in which we experience the other as a true gift. I told Diana of my delight in the seemingly boundless energy and determination she exhibits in tackling her many family projects. I told her of the way in which her playfulness often frees me to let go of my own obsession with social propriety. She in turn thanked me for my commitment to see that our family comes before my career and for my conscientiousness regarding the value of making joint family decisions. The dinner was an experience of authentic mutuality as we gratefully affirmed the gifts we shared with one another in our marriage.

Much of the shared communion of married life is sustained by this dynamic whereby we both receive gifts from our spouses and receive our spouses as gifts themselves. By definition, this sense of gift cannot be quantified and measured. Nothing kills a marriage like that deadly game of marital accounting where each keeps track of the "things done for the other" with the never quite spoken expectation of reciprocation. Yet how could I possibly quantify gifts my wife offers me? I am blessed when a night ending in argument is followed by a day begun anew with a kiss. I am blessed when I return home from work venting my frustrations on my wife and yet still find myself loved and accepted. I can only receive as pure gift the forgiveness offered again and again in response to my own pettiness and hardness of heart. These gifts cannot be quantified in view of compensation. No, the return gift I offer my spouse belongs not within the realm of economic equivalency but that of grace and blessing.

The offering and receiving of gifts lies at the heart of two central Christian affirmations: the Trinity and the paschal mystery. The doctrine of the Trinity reveals a "gifting God" who gives out of the depths of divine love without ever being depleted. The paschal mystery gives concrete shape to this divine gift as Jesus lived a life of self-bestowal before others. Indeed, in Jesus God displayed the deep logic of gift in the most radical form possible: the offer of one's life for another.

When my spouse and I enter the logic of gift, by what we offer to and receive from one another, we both discover our truest selves in the mutuality of our relationship and enter into the realm of the divine, where we draw from and add to "the momentum of God's giving."[15]

There is an element of delight in the experience of mutuality. There are times when I will sneak upstairs and listen quietly to Diana reading to one of our children. I catch myself grinning as I savor the enthusiasm and energy that she puts into reading these stories. At other times delight gives way to pure and simple pride. I recall the way I felt when Diana finally received her graduate degree, thinking back on those many late nights when I would go to bed while she stayed up studying. Surely these moments — when we find ourselves drawn out of our own world to delight in our beloved and his or her accomplishments, when we attend to our spouse not as an object but as gift — shape us in unseen ways.

Authentic mutuality within marriage would seem to exclude the hierarchical view of the marriage relationship often advocated by fundamentalist Christians. I am convinced that hierarchically structured marriages can manifest authentic marital love and a real reciprocity, that is, a sense that marriage entails binding obligations for both parties. However, it is difficult to recognize in these marriage relationships true mutuality, for if mutuality involves the acknowledgment of gifts, hierarchical notions of the marriage relationship ask one partner, the wife, to suppress some of her gifts in deference to her spouse.

I will admit that often these marriages flourish, as both spouses engage in a form of authentic marital love and respect within this traditional structure. We lived for several years next door to a devout evangelical Christian family in which

the husband and wife firmly believed in the hierarchical structure of marriage as divinely sanctioned. I do not question the
sanctity of their relationship nor would I deny that both exhib-
ited a profound love and respect for one another. But I do find
myself wondering whether part of the reason their marriage
worked lay less in the purported divine source of this arrangement than in the natural differentiation in their personalities
such that each was already inclined by personal temperament
to a particular role in the marriage. She flourished in her
wide-ranging domestic responsibilities as he naturally assumed
the financial and disciplinary responsibilities conventionally
assigned to the male of the household.

But what happens when the natural dispositions of the
spouses do not follow these "divinely sanctioned" roles? What
happens when the husband possesses few career aspirations
and finds his greatest satisfaction in domestic life? What happens when the wife seeks to pursue a professional career
requiring a considerable investment of time and energy? What
happens when couples find that they function best when all
significant family decisions are made jointly rather than by
one or the other functioning as head? Are such couples to be
viewed as a spiritual aberration?

There are certainly times when I envy our former neighbors. When we both worked full time, Diana and I had to get
up each morning and, in significant ways, reinvent our relationship. We had to decide who picks up the kids and takes
them to baseball practice. We had to negotiate who would
have to take off work to bring one of them to a doctor's appointment. These decisions were by no means free of conflict,
and at times the process was downright wearying. Our life together would doubtless be easier if we had entered into some
clear contractual agreements on our wedding day (though I

suspect that more men than women would agree with me on this): "You will have all responsibilities for the kids' health and education; I will provide financial security for our family." But I also believe that such a contractual arrangement, particularly if it was made under the shadow of some vague divine sanction (e.g., "this is what Christian wives are supposed to do"), brings with it serious risks. It can give rise to that deadly mixture of guilt and resentment by one or both spouses. Too often the result will be a dangerous and potentially corrosive inequity in the assignment of family responsibilities.

Of course couples do enter into pragmatic agreements regarding the conduct of their life together. Frequently one person will have a better head for finances; another will derive more satisfaction from cooking. Often one will have very strong convictions about the kind of neighborhood they should live in while the other might feel much stronger about how family leisure time ought to be spent. What makes these agreements *mutual* is that they proceed from a shared discernment of gifts and obligations. It is when agreements about marital or familial roles are viewed as if etched on stone tablets by God that the mutuality of the relationship is threatened.

I once worked with a colleague who was having a disagreement with her spouse over their children's education. The husband felt they should attend a Catholic school, while she was convinced the local public school offered a better overall education and that the couple together, both committed Catholics, could provide adequately for the children's Christian formation. He eventually deferred to her because he knew she was both better informed on the matter (she had personally visited both schools, interviewing teachers and examining curricula) and much more passionately committed to her viewpoint than he was to his. In another situation it might well be the wife who would defer. The point is that deference to the other emerges out of love and respect for one's spouse and not out of some social expectation or reluctant accommodation.

There are solid reasons for holding that the view that this hierarchical structure is divinely sanctioned depends less on biblical warrants and more on a fundamentalist interpretation of certain key biblical passages. It is true that St. Paul seems to have accepted certain cultural assumptions about women in, for example, 1 Corinthians 11:3–16, in which he argues that women ought to keep their heads veiled when in prayer. Paul accepts the dominant cultural hierarchy, which asserts male superiority over women. This passage is an admonishment to the Corinthians who may have been flouting certain social conventions in the behavior of female church members. Paul argues in support of these social conventions, but his main point is to use this accepted hierarchical structure as a device for asserting Christ's relationship to the church. Another text, likely to have been written by a disciple of Paul, is found in the letter to the Ephesians and is perhaps the strongest biblical text in support of a hierarchical structure in marriage. This passage also likely represents some of the dominant cultural assumptions of the time. Yet upon closer examination the text may also be revising at least part of those larger cultural assumptions about the superiority of the husband in the marriage relationship. Let us consider the crucial text (Eph. 5:21–32):

> Be subordinate to one another out of reverence for Christ. Wives should be subordinate to their husbands as to the Lord. For the husband is head of his wife just as Christ is head of the church, he himself the savior

of the body. As the church is subordinate to Christ, so wives should be subordinate to their husbands in everything. Husbands, love your wives, even as Christ loved the church and handed himself over for her to sanctify her, cleansing her by the bath of water with the word, that he might present to himself the church in splendor, without spot or wrinkle or any such thing, that she might be holy and without blemish. So [also] husbands should love their wives as their own bodies. He who loves his wife loves himself. For no one hates his own flesh but rather nourishes and cherishes it, even as Christ does the church, because we are members of his body. "For this reason a man shall leave [his] father and [his] mother and be joined to his wife, and the two shall become one flesh." This is a great mystery, but I speak in reference to Christ and the church. In any case, each one of you should love his wife as himself, and the wife should respect her husband.

This passage is often misinterpreted because of the statement that just as Christ is head of the church, so too the husband is to be head of the wife.[16] In fact, while the sexist overtones cannot be completely overlooked, this passage is much more subtle than is generally realized and challenges traditional notions of the subordination of the wife. First, the passage begins with a call to *mutual subordination* one to the other. Only after this call to mutual subordination is male headship asserted. Even then this headship is reinterpreted. The author says "the husband is the head of the wife as Christ is the head of the church." The husband's headship over the wife was a virtually universal presupposition in the Mediterranean cultures of the late first century. Yet the author of this text is taking an accepted attitude and turning it on its head. The point that seems to be made is that, for Christians, the headship of the husband is to be modeled on the headship of Christ, not on secular notions of headship. The consistent biblical testimony regarding Christ's headship is that it was not one of secular lordship, but rather one of self-effacing service ("The Son of Man came not to be served but to serve"). It is in this sense that the husband is to exercise "headship." This suggests that the husband is being encouraged not to be a head over the wife in the larger cultural understanding as that of superiority and domination, but rather in accord with Christ — to exercise headship as humble service. The husband is to be the "first servant of the wife."[17]

The overarching thrust of the text is to ground marriage in a covenant fidelity characterized by a love that is understood, not as mere interpersonal affection, but as a mutual "giving oneself away" to the other. This sense of marital covenant is also evident in Jesus' own prohibition of divorce (see Matt. 19:3–12). It is a prohibition that essentially rejects the Mosaic law's allowance for a husband divorcing his wife (but not the reverse). Jesus' condemnation of divorce affirms the covenantal character of marriage while at the same time suggesting that the wife is not to be viewed any longer as mere chattel to be dispensed with as the husband wishes.

Intimacy

The life of marital communion is constituted not only by the experience of mutuality as we learn to delight in and affirm the gifts our spouses offer us, but also in the experience of intimacy. I will discuss sexual intimacy in a later chapter; here it will suffice to speak of the broader experience of intimacy in marriage. We tend to think of intimacy as an expression of emotional closeness between two people, yet this is not quite correct. Marital intimacy is nurtured when we strive to go beyond a desire for closeness to a genuine vulnerability before one another. It is what happens when I risk opening up my deepest concerns and fears to another. It occurs when two people risk sharing plans and dreams, rejoicing together when they are realized and mourning when they are dashed. This vulnerability is what gives to human intimacy its power. But as is always the case with power, there are risks involved.

To draw close to another is not only to affect the other but to be open to being affected by the other. I have learned much from James and Evelyn Whitehead's insightful treatment of this. They note that authentic intimacy requires that those being intimate have sufficiently developed selves. Few things are more dangerous than a person with an insufficiently developed personal identity entering into an intimate relationship with another. The risk, in such situations, is that the undeveloped self will not only be affected by the other, but will be lost in the other. As the Whiteheads point out:

> Without a clear sense of who I am, I have little to bring to our relationship. There is no "me" to give to the process of mutual confirmation and growth. Instead, I try to become what you want me to be, or what I *think* you want me to be.[18]

This is the difficulty with the false conception of marital unity as that of two halves together comprising a whole. Unity is not absorption. Authentic communion occurs in expressions of intimacy not when one is absorbed into the other nor completed by the other, nor when one submits to the images, fantasies, and expectations of the other, but when two unique selves freely give themselves over in communion with the other. Intimacy is a powerful reality, and it can "annihilate" an immature self without a sufficiently developed personal identity. It is one thing for me to enter into intimate communion with the other with the full knowledge that I am likely to be changed by that encounter. It is another thing altogether to enter into intimate communion with another and lose my sense of self in the process. Authentic marital communion in intimacy is neither the merger of two selves nor the absorption of one self into the other; it is the abiding together of two persons whose identities are both affirmed and transformed as they offer themselves as gift to the other.

I recall an incident several years ago in which I encountered a woman whom I had known as a friend in college. My memory of her was of a bright and enthusiastic person with a remarkable intellect. I recall her genuine love for college life, not so much for the social interactions it offered as for the opportunities for learning. She was intoxicated by the life of the mind. In the courses we had together, she was never content to do the assigned reading but would do all of the optional reading as well and, invariably, she would offer the most insightful comments in class discussion. Each semester she handled with ease a course load that would have crushed me.

I bumped into her at an airport one day, some ten years later. As we chatted, catching up on each other's lives, I could not help noticing how much she had changed. I am not speaking of her physical appearance but of the vitality and energy that had once radiated from her as she engaged in her academic pursuits. In the course of our conversation I learned that about six months after I had last seen her, she met her future husband, fell in love, dropped out of school, and got married. Her husband had strong feelings about the importance of his being the "breadwinner" and insisted that she neither continue her studies nor get a job. Within months of their wedding she became pregnant. She showed me pictures of her children with obvious pride and love. Still, I could not shake the sense that she was not content in her life.

Now there is nothing wrong with those who decide that college is not for them. Nor is there anything wrong in a woman (or a man, for that matter) deciding to forsake a professional career in favor of being a full-time housekeeper. There is a problem, however, when people with an obvious love for academics and learning abandon all that gives them joy in life out of devotion to another. Is it possible that, lacking a sufficiently developed sense of self, she ended up abandoning that which most fulfilled her to be what someone else, her future spouse, wanted her to be?

The other possibility, equally resistant to authentic intimacy, occurs with individuals who possess an overly rigid self-definition. In this situation I become incapable of intimacy because of an unwillingness to undergo the changes that real intimacy demands:

> There is too little flexibility in my sense of who I am, too little openness to learn something new about myself or to change. Personal rigidity leaves little room for self-exploration or self-disclosure. And without self-exploration and self-disclosure I cannot move beyond myself toward you.[19]

The sad truth is that very often those belonging to the second category will seek out for mates those in the first category, and vice versa. Those unwilling to change are naturally going to be drawn to those only too ready to give up their own identity for another.

The experience of true intimacy is one of the greatest gifts of married life. In this intimacy I experience my wife as the one person who knows my deepest fears and stands ready as a "balm for my wounds."[20] I remember early in my teaching career when the annual ritual of reading students' course evaluations would be met with dread. I might receive twenty positive evaluations only to be devastated by the two negative critiques. My colleagues would often laugh at my consternation. Then I would call my wife and read them to her, sensing with relief that at least she knew of the hidden wounds I carried that inclined me to give a disproportionate weight to these few negative comments. Indeed, it is a blessed comfort to know that this other person, whose own story began long before I appeared in her life, has chosen to weave her story inextricably into mine such that we become together co-authors of some broken but cherished verse.

Although intimacy is concerned with our capacity to be close to another, this closeness is not always a positive or pleasant experience. To be in an intimate relationship is to submit yourself to the discomfort of confrontation. The intimacy of marriage means having someone always "in your face" calling you to growth. It also may mean sharing the pain of another.

People are often surprised when I tell them that one of the most intimate moments in our marriage came when we experienced the loss of our first child *in utero*. We had discovered that we were pregnant in February. In mid-May, the day before we were to leave for a trip to Europe, we went in for a checkup, and the doctor was disturbed that she could not detect a heart beat. We went for a sonogram and learned that the baby had died probably about a month earlier. Diana would have to return to the hospital later that evening to

have the dead infant safely removed from her womb, a pro-
cedure normally associated with abortion. I still recall being
with Diana in the hospital room after the radiologist had left
us alone, staring at the frozen image of our baby still on the
screen. Diana went up to the screen and silently traced the
cross on the image, and we both began to cry. Marital communion manifested itself in the tortured intimacy of two broken
hearts finding solace in one another.

What marital intimacy, in all its forms, shares is an openness to an experience of love and acceptance that is ultimately
supernatural in origin even as it comes to us in human form.
To be in a committed, intimate relationship is to clear that
space in one's heart for another, a space that becomes at the
same time an interior temple in which God abides.

Companionship

To marry another is not just to acquire a sexual partner or
a lover; it is to discover a companion. There is much to be
learned from considering one's spouse as a companion. The
word derives from the Latin prefix *com-* or "with" and *panis* or
"bread." A *companio* is one with whom a person shares bread.

Bread is an ancient symbol suggesting both the fruit of
human labor and the stuff of human nourishment. It is a
powerful biblical image. God offers the biblical bread, manna,
to feed Moses and the Israelites wandering in the desert. Yet
the gift of manna required the Israelites to rise each morning
to gather the manna. When they tried to store the manna to
avoid the daily chore of rising and gathering the bread, the
manna rotted. God's provision had to be patiently received
daily as gift, not hoarded and controlled. On the one hand,
Jesus was tempted in the desert to turn stones into bread but

resisted, knowing that bread produced with the snap of fingers for one's own sustenance is no longer gift. On the other hand, the multiplication of bread was one of Jesus' most characteristic wonders, demonstrating the superabundant generosity of God. And, of course, at the last supper Jesus identifies himself with bread, becoming food for the world.

To see my spouse as a companion is to see her as one who shares bread with me. This means, in the first place, that in marriage we are to nourish one another. There is a faint echo of this profound commitment enacted at weddings when the newly married feed each other a piece of the wedding cake. This ceremonial action discloses an often unnoted foreshadowing of married life.

Diana once participated in a chaplaincy internship in an institutional home for the elderly. While there she befriended a resident, Fred, who was partially paralyzed and was visited regularly by his wife, Josie. She was no longer able to care for him on her own, but she came daily to visit. His pride always led him to fuss at the nurses as they attempted to feed him, but when his wife arrived, he docilely accepted her ministrations. Diana was quite moved by the sight of Josie gently cutting Fred's food and feeding him bite by bite. The tender companionship of marriage was being enacted before her eyes in its most spare and vital form. Yet throughout the life of a marriage husband and wife are called upon, often at considerable sacrifice, to nourish one another. We are invited to identify the needs of our spouses and, where necessary, to respond to them.

Diana recently worked in a situation in which she felt she was being treated unfairly by one of her colleagues. I would become enraged when she would report various incidents to me, and I had to resist the temptation to march into her workplace and settle the problem myself. However, having made this mistake once before, I had finally learned enough about myself to recognize the dysfunctional character of this kind of action. Besides, at heart I knew that my wife was a strong and able woman quite capable of fighting her own battles. The "bread" she needed from me was empathy and emotional support.

The quality of companionship possible for a couple is likely to change over the years of their marriage. As I reflect on the married couples I have had the opportunity to know over the years, I am struck by the changing rhythms of their marriages. If you listen to the narratives of couples married less than fifteen years or so, a common feature seems to emerge. The emotional rhythm in the marriage often oscillates dramatically. That is, a couple might experience an extended period in which everything just feels right about their relationship. There are fewer arguments, intimacy and understanding comes easily, temptations and distractions are few. However this period will then be followed by another, filled with difficulty and conflict. During these times the relationship can feel empty and lifeless. One of the challenges couples face during these years of marriage is that of accepting this rhythm, celebrating the seasons of closeness while not overreacting to the wintry seasons. The good news is that a distinguishing mark of mature, successful marriages is a gradual diminishment of such dramatic swings in the mood of the relationship. The trust gained from decades of negotiating their common commitment levels out to some extent the seasonal rhythms of their marriage. The result is gentler peaks and valleys.

I have tried to describe in this chapter some of the salient characteristics of the life of communion for married couples. This life of communion manifests itself in the human experiences of mutuality, intimacy, and companionship. It is here, in the warp and woof of married life that spouses experience the grace of God. Marriage is not "made holy" merely by injecting moments of formal prayer into one's life or hanging crucifixes over one's marital bed. While prayer is vital for cultivating our conscious awareness of God's presence, the graced character of our marriage is found not primarily on our knees but in the events of communion patiently nurtured in the committed loving relationship between husband and wife.

Questions for Reflection and Discussion

1. In your marriage, how have you cultivated the mutuality of marital communion? What are the gifts that your spouse offers you in marriage?

2. Are there obstacles that have made it difficult for you to risk being vulnerable with your spouse?

3. How have you nurtured companionship in your marriage? What is the "bread" that you and your spouse share?

Chapter Three

Marriage and Conversion

Recent studies confirm that Americans are getting married at a much later age than generations past and for different reasons. Still, most Americans do view marriage as part of life's natural progression; the vast majority of us will marry at some point in our lives. However, when I contemplated the decision to marry over a decade ago, it felt like anything but a natural progression. I was thirty years old, almost two years into a steady, contented relationship with an intelligent, athletic, and attractive young woman. Clearly the time was coming to make some decisions about our future together. I sensed that if I was ever going to marry this was the time and this was the woman. Still, somewhat hesitant to make a commitment, I sought out a good friend who had been married for several years. Having exhausted our sports related "guy talk" over a Wendy's hamburger, I began awkwardly. "Rob, was there any one thing that was significant in helping you decide to marry Nancy?" There was simply no way to make a smooth transition to this kind of a question, and I immediately felt embarrassed for posing it. Yet before I could backtrack, he shot back his answer with a confidence that made me wonder whether he had been waiting for me to broach the subject. "She was my salvation." His response, frankly, made

me uncomfortable, and I dismissed it. Now, a little over a
decade into marriage, I find myself entertaining his answer in
a new light.

I am growing in the conviction that my relationship with
my wife and my children is indeed the spiritual "place"
wherein I will work out my salvation. Of course salvation
is always God's work. Yet at least the Catholic Christian tradition insists that there is a kind of cooperation in our free
response to God's grace. Put simply, while salvation is always
God's work in us and therefore a free gift, it often *feels* like our
work as we struggle to remain open to God's saving action.
In any event, I have become convinced that my "salvation,"
the spiritual transformation that God wishes to effect in me,
transpires within the crucible of my relationship with my wife
and children. I experience this saving work in different ways.
Like most married people, there are times when I find myself
overwhelmed with gratitude for the shared life I have with my
wife. At other times marriage presents itself as an invitation
to that difficult yet necessary paschal movement from life to
death to new life.

Call to Conversion

In her perceptive meditations on marriage, Nancy Mairs
contends that marriage is fundamentally an invitation to
conversion:

> This [the marriage commitment] was, and has remained,
> the paradigmatic conversion, infinitely more powerful
> and penetrating than anything connected with exclu-
> sively religious conviction or practice. I might have
> found another way to God. I might have found a better

way to God. But I did not. My spirit has been schooled in wedlock.[21]

This linkage of marriage and conversion is striking. The biblical word for conversion, *metanoia,* means not just a shift in one's views or opinions but a fundamental change in direction. Marriage, Mairs contends, demands change at the very core of one's being. From the perspective of Christian faith, it is a call to enter into the paschal mystery, that sacred rhythm of life-death-life.

I had a very dear friend, Mary, who died of cancer while still in her thirties. I recall a frank conversation we shared about three months before she died. I asked her how her faith helped her to prepare for what we both knew lay ahead. She said something quite remarkable:

> There are times, Rick, when I am embarrassed to admit how frequently my faith gives way in the face of doubt. I have had moments when I wasn't sure I believed in Christ's divinity, or his real presence in the eucharist, or even in the Trinity itself. But through all of these times of doubt, there is one thing I have never questioned, and that is that the paschal mystery, the paradoxical logic that tells us that we find life only in dying, is the one indispensable key to unlocking the universe. In the midst of a thousand doubts I have always clung to the witness of Jesus that there can be no rising without dying.

Mary did not fear her approaching death because she had embraced death, not as the final punctuation mark to her life story but as a raw fact of her daily existence. I have affirmed the importance of the life of communion to which all are called. Yet this life of communion can be fully realized, as

Mary taught me, only when we are willing to enter into the paschal movement of dying and rising.

Marriage and the Paschal Mystery

Marriage, like all sacraments, is paschal to the core, and consequently it is as much about dying as it is about new life. We do not get much of this on television. There is plenty of marital dying, to be sure, but it is usually a foreshadowing of some quick marital exit. Paschal "dying" is an altogether different matter. The widespread romanticization of love and marriage (and both church and society have contributed in their own ways to this romanticization) has done much to obscure the paschal character of Christian marriage. Yet it is virtually impossible for a marriage to survive the inevitable tests, obstacles, and challenges that will come before it unless the couple grasps the paschal character of their endeavor.

Consider the relatively common experience in marriage of being misunderstood. When I have an argument with my colleagues at work, I can always leave the workplace and the discomfort that the disagreement generated. I can go home, grouse about the dispute a bit with my wife, and then take refuge in my family life, emotionally far removed from my job. In marriage, it is much harder to find refuge from misunderstanding, disagreement, or conflict. I may storm out of the house after a heated argument with my wife, but I have to return eventually. The source of disagreement and the experience of being misunderstood cannot be avoided with the ease that I can avoid the discomfort of the workplace. Moreover, the experience of deep misunderstanding in marriage is quite different from the experience of disagreement or conflict with colleagues in the workplace. For one thing, my expectations for marriage are much higher. After all, I did not accept my job expecting that all of my colleagues would become my "best buddies." I did not take the job expecting that my colleagues would be an emotional salve when I am hurt or an anchor for me in times of doubt. The evaluation of my job performance rarely takes into account whether I have offered my assistant a sympathetic ear.

In marriage, however, these are precisely the things I expect of my partner, and when they are not present in our marriage, the pain and loss is acute. If the sexual intimacy of marriage is a most tender grace, the experience of sharing a marriage bed with one who at this particular moment may *not* understand me can be terrifying in its loneliness. As Ronald Rolheiser put it, "It is painful to sleep alone but it is perhaps more painful to sleep alone when you are not sleeping alone."[22] There is a paschal "dying" that married couples have to embrace in the inevitable experience of loneliness that misunderstanding, disagreement, or conflict brings.

In spite of our closeness, my wife and I view our shared world in notably different ways. It is not that our values are different, but rather that we construe events differently and give a distinct priority to the tasks we face. Let me offer a fairly trivial example. My own penchant for order leads me systematically to take on the least pleasant projects first in my life. I have to complete all outstanding tasks before I can allow myself the pleasure of relaxation. For example, when we return from a trip I must unpack all of my bags before I can flop on the bed and rest. My wife, however, will unpack her bag when she actually *needs* those clothes! She possesses a unique capacity to enjoy the present moment, putting aside all but the most necessary of tasks for another time. At the same time, it also means that she tends to leave a lot of tasks unfinished. Her still packed suitcase might sit in the middle of our bedroom for several weeks. It would be easy to speak of this kind of difference as an experience of "complementarity" in our marriage relationship, but in point of fact we usually experience it as an irritating difference, pure and simple. In my lesser moments I am wholly convinced that Diana's life would be happier and more fulfilling if she would adopt more of my attitude toward life. Over a decade into marriage, I still harbor this illusion that she is my own personal "work in progress" and still fancy that she will eventually come around to the inherent superiority of my point of view! I feel confident that she holds similar views about me.

These differences between us may in fact be the very nodal point of my conversion. The place of difference and disagreement is the spiritual place in which I am called to a kind of dying, to a vulnerability in which I must try to enter sympathetically into *her* perspective. I am called, without rejecting all that I value, to put aside, if only for a moment, all of my treasured competencies and proven ways of doing things and entertain her viewpoint. This is a risky venture for me precisely because so much of my self-worth is wrapped up in assumptions about the intrinsic superiority of my worldview. This experience of being stretched by the otherness of one's spouse is, I am convinced, an experience of nothing less than God's saving work in us.

The possibility of conversion occurs in these experiences of misunderstanding and the clashes that develop as we discover that we often construe our lives in very different ways. Each of us brings into our marriage private wounds and habits of relating that will need to be challenged. The vocation of marriage is indeed a calling (the root meaning of "vocation") to be stretched, drawn out to an emotional and relational "far country." There is a biblical term for what is demanded here, *kenosis*. St. Paul used the term to describe what it was for Christ to abandon all divine prerogatives in order to enter fully into the experience of being human. For those of us who fulfill our baptismal call to follow Jesus in and through the sacrament of matrimony, *kenosis* is the call to a self-emptying or dying to our own needs, hopes, and expectations. It is also a call to attend to this person who, at any given moment, can appear to me not just as gift but as disturbingly *other*. This is one of the great paradoxes of marriage — a relationship so often sought because of the intimacy it offers in fact can confront us not with the closeness of our partner but with our partner's shocking *otherness*. I am challenged to view my wife not as a cipher to be decoded but as a person to be embraced as mystery.

Marriage as an Ascetical Vocation

The faithful living of matrimonial vows involves an elemental redirection away from that which is most typical of a single person's life, the opportunity to explore the breadth of experience that life has to offer. So often, particularly for males, I suspect, the fear of commitment is grounded in the recognition that there is a breadth of human experience that may well no longer be available in marriage. I may no longer be free to decide at the last moment to spend a summer in Europe hiking with some college buddies. I certainly will no longer be able to ask an attractive woman I meet at a party for her phone number.

In marriage, as with any ascetical practice, there is a free renunciation of goods. Frankly, I do not believe enough is said about this. When I was growing up attending Catholic schools, the teachers would often speak of three possible vocations, priesthood (though only the boys were presented with this option!), consecrated religious life (life as a "sister" or "brother"), or marriage. The single life, regrettably, was not viewed as a distinct vocation, but merely an interim state prior to committing to one of the three basic options. As the three vocational alternatives were generally presented, marriage was associated with parenthood and spousal intimacy, while the priesthood and consecrated religious life were presented as the more heroic options because of the renunciation of goods (most notable by way of celibacy) associated with them.

I believe that marriage involves spouses in a way of life that has more in common with the vowed life of consecrated religious than is generally realized. This is because, as married persons, we too have entered into a vowed life. It draws us as well into a permanent public commitment to enter into the paschal mystery through a real renunciation of goods. Those who would consider marriage survey the wide range of possible human relationships in which the many blessings of human and sexual intimacy may be found and renounce them in favor of the exclusive marital intimacy to be cultivated with their spouse. This is a freely chosen limitation and might be charac-terized as a choice to explore the *depth* of human experience with this one person over the *breadth* of human experience that can be explored prior to a marital commitment. When I marry, I make a free choice to forsake the possibility of explor-ing the same kind of intimate relationship with any number of different persons in exchange for the unique relationship I will have with my spouse.

While each spouse brings significant personal gifts to a mar-riage, those gifts are finite and in time each spouse will become aware, often painfully aware, of what the other partner does not and cannot bring. For every time that one's spouse is graciously present and attentive in a time of need, there will be a time of real or emotional absence. In marriage, and particularly in marriage with children, spouses are confronted every moment of their lives with claims made upon them by others: claims on time, finances, affection, and simple attentiveness. Prior to marriage, we experienced a certain freedom to bestow our time, finances, affection, and attentiveness on those we chose when we chose. In marriage, however, claims can and are made on what was once subject to the free disposition of the individual. Bills come in, children need to be diapered at 3:00 a.m., a spouse needs to talk about the events of the day. The spirituality of marriage is shaped by one's response to these claims.

An adequate Christian understanding of marriage must emphasize the sacramental significance, not only of marital intimacy but of this sense of absence, longing, and the embrace of the limits of the relationship. When this sense of lack or absence is not embraced, the result is often infidelity. Infidelity takes many forms. It may be expressed as actual adultery or through the many "small exits" by which we avoid the inevitable experiences of emptiness, disappointment, and longing. These "small exits" can include something as serious as alchoholism and substance abuse or something as seemingly innocuous as television, sports, working out at the gym, a bridge club, or children's activities. These activities, many of which can be legitimate in themselves, risk becoming ways to escape the relationship and thereby avoid the emptiness and loneliness that married life occasionally will bring.

I once had a friend who some years ago shared with me some of his struggles regarding his marital commitment. He had graduated from law school as a brilliant and promising lawyer. His professional future was bright. Then he married, and he and his wife had several children. He came to realize that if he was to fulfill his responsibilities to his wife and children he would not be able to put the time into his career that he had once hoped. He had to let go of the dream of ever becoming a partner in his firm. This was a bitter pill for him to swallow because he knew that he did not lack either the ability or the drive. He began to see a therapist, and at one point she asked him a curious question: Did he have a bachelor's party with his friends on the eve of his wedding? He was puzzled by the question but admitted that, no, he had not. He and his wife believed that such parties tended to be sexist and suggested a negative view of marriage as a "ball and chain." Consequently, the couple decided to have a joint party with their best friends.

The therapist gently suggested that this decision might have been a mistake. The importance of such parties, she contended, is that they can help us honestly mourn the passing of a life that we will have no more. This does not mean that we embrace the view that our spouse will be a "ball and chain." It does mean, she contended, ritually acknowledging with friends that a way of life, a life full of unlimited choice and the widest possible range of human experience, will now be renounced. In its place the soon-to-be-married person will now begin a new life constituted by a vital life commitment to one other person and the children that may issue from that relationship.

In the early church those who were executed because of their Christian faith were called *martyres*, those whose deaths offered a profound and dramatic testimony to the Christian way of life as a free entrance into the dying and rising of Christ. As widespread Christian persecution died out, the dramatic witness of the early martyrs eventually gave way to the asceticism of monastic and consecrated religious life. Those who embraced the public profession of the evangelical counsels interpreted the significance of their lives in the light of the *kenosis,* or self-emptying, of Christ. To make vows of poverty, chastity, and obedience was to freely accept the limitations that these vows imposed, but it was also to recognize that through this free embrace would come life eternal. If Christian asceticism often has been associated with unhealthy exercises in self-mortification, the essential truth was nevertheless preserved that in the Christian life, pain, suffering, emptiness, loneliness, and even boredom — the so-called negative characteristics of human existence — must be embraced as part of the fabric of our lives. Moreover, only through the free embrace of these negativities of human existence could life's graciousness likewise be embraced. When spouses freely accept the limits of the marital relationship, when they choose to love even out of the emptiness, they enter into the paschal rhythm of life-death-life and work out their salvation.

This view of Christian marriage challenges basic North American cultural assumptions. We live in a consumerist culture that often measures cultural progress in terms of the expansion of choices available to us. If cable television offers us access to fifty television channels but a satellite dish can make over a hundred different viewing choices available we see it as almost self-evident that, all things being equal, we would prefer the satellite's expanded offerings. If the corner grocery offered us all of the basic food staples necessary to meet our nutritional needs in a context that allowed for familiarity with our grocer and regular interaction with our neighbors, it still could not compete with the latest supermarket's dramatically expanded grocery offerings. If modern cultural patterns are any indication, Americans will generally opt for the maximization of choice over the intangible benefits of shopping at a corner grocery. The Tom Hanks/Meg Ryan movie *You've Got Mail* made this point as it pitted the huge, antiseptic mega-bookstore against the small neighborhood specialty bookstore. The value of vastly expanded choice trumped the intangible delights of lingering in a specialty shop run by a proprietor who knew and loved books.

Alongside this consumerist obsession with expanding the range of choices available to us is our growing preoccupation with technological disburdenment.[23] Modern technology offers us the goods we desire without the effort that had once been necessary to procure those goods. Consider our changing relationship to music. If we had lived in 1902 rather than 2002, a love for music would normally have led us to take up the discipline of making music either through singing or playing a musical instrument. Today the modern recording industry has made music ubiquitous; we hear it in the doctor's waiting room, when we are put on hold, in our cars on our daily commute, or anywhere we wish if we carry with us a portable CD player. The precious good of music acquired only by discipline and effort has now become a carefully packaged commodity. The microwave oven offers us a nominally nourishing meal without the time-consuming effort that a home-cooked meal demands. Technology offers us the goods we desire without effort or burden.

We must consider the consequences for marriage of this cultural preoccupation with the maximization of choice and the view that burden and effort are realities to be technologically overcome. When we are encouraged to trade in our car every few years for a newer model, does not this mentality influence us when we experience the inevitable difficulties that commitment to any one individual will entail? Is not the flourishing pornography industry but the logical consequence of the technological tendency to offer us the goods we desire (in this case the delights of sexual pleasure) purged of all of the depth, texture, and "friction" that comes with any meaningful human relationship? Christian convictions about marriage must challenge the growing cultural assumption that marriage is simply one more consumer choice.[24]

"You Always Marry the Wrong Person"

I know a college theology professor who has a reputation for beginning his course on the sacrament of marriage each semester by saying: "It is a fundamental axiom of marriage that we always marry the wrong person." The statement was guaranteed to shock the students, but it contained a profound insight. There is a pervasive myth in our culture, fueled by Hollywood and television, that somewhere out there is the perfect partner for us. We choose our future mate out of the conviction that he or she is that "right person." And for a time the intoxication of romance and the highly erotic charge of our initial sexual attraction to our beloved confirms the "rightness" of our betrothed. But over time, as the flush of the initial romance fades in the early years of marriage, the onset of children may dampen the opportunities for spousal intimacy and spontaneity. Sexual familiarity replaces the erotic charge of the honeymoon, and one's convictions about the "rightness" of one's spouse begin to be questioned. As basic marital expectations and relational needs go unmet, one or both begin to wonder whether or not a "mistake" was made in their choice of their spouse. Quite often a third party arrives on the scene, possessing all the qualities lacking in one's spouse, and now the third party is seen as the "right person" and one's spouse as the "wrong person."

The National Marriage Project, associated with Rutgers University, in its latest report, *The State of Our Unions — 2001*, confirms this suspicion. In their report on the attitudes that those in their twenties have about marriage today they reveal that "the overwhelming majority (94 percent) of never married singles agree that 'when you marry you want your spouse to be your soul mate, first and foremost.'" Almost as large a majority (88 percent) agree that "there is a special person, a soul mate, waiting for you somewhere out there." The authors of the study express concern that "the centuries-old ideal of friendship in marriage, or what sociologists call companionate marriage, may be evolving into a more exalted and demanding standard of a spiritualized union of souls." It is a not altogether surprising reaction to the divorce culture in which these young people have been raised, but, the authors fear, "the soul mate ideal of marriage may create unrealistic expectations that, if unfulfilled, may lead to marital discontent and perhaps search for a new soul mate."

Our professor's axiom suggests that engaged couples would do better to enter into their commitment with a steely-eyed understanding that in some sense they are "marrying the wrong person" and that this reality in no way undermines the legitimacy of this marriage. Indeed, the acceptance of the seeming "wrongness" of one's spouse can provide the opportunity for transformation and growth. (Let me hasten to add that the "wrongness" of one's spouse that I have in mind is not at all to be confused with the wrongness of an abusive spouse — a situation that should never be simply tolerated or endured.)

There is a line of thought in marriage and family therapy that would seem to confirm this insight. The noted expert in marriage therapy Augustus Napier, in his book *The Fragile Bond*, suggests that we are motivated in our choice of marriage partner by the highly idealized image of the "good parent" that we constructed long ago in our early childhood.[25] This theory is far removed from the simplistic "males try to marry a woman like their mother" and "females try to marry a man like their father." The theory has it that all of us face fundamental issues growing up in our family of origin. Not all of these issues are fully resolved in our childhood. For some of us the issue was about self-esteem and acceptance; for others it was about dealing with authority. The point is that when we marry, at a deep and rarely conscious level, we seek someone who will help us address these issues. We look to our would-be spouse as the magic partner who will heal our wounds. Thus, the core issues of our childhood are, as likely as not, to be reenacted in our marriage

> ... because of the person we have chosen to marry; for we seem powerfully drawn to marry someone who will help us recapitulate those early struggles with our parents. We may think we are marrying someone very different from our parents ... but the likelihood is that we will find ourselves forced to deal in our marriage with the core themes and struggles of our early life.[26]

This is not a bad thing, Napier insists, because we enter into this relationship in the hope, not merely of reenacting childhood conflicts, but of healing them. My spouse gives me an opportunity to develop an alternative pattern of response to that which I adopted as a child. Now the irony of this situation is that at some point, when the reenactment of childhood conflicts occurs and our spouse begins to act alarmingly like our primary caregivers of long ago, we immediately assume that we made a mistake. We recall acutely the pain of such conflicts in our past, and we do not want to experience that pain again. When our spouse refuses to change we are inclined to assume that he or she is not "right" for us. We fail to recognize that this situation is precisely the opportunity that, at an unconscious level, we sought when we chose our spouse in the first place. It is an opportunity to change not our spouses but ourselves, to become persons capable of responding differently to a painful situation. The possibility for change and growth comes only when we acknowledge that the primary source of our growing unhappiness in the marriage lies not with our spouse but with our own unresolved issues.

Let me offer a personal example of this dynamic. I was raised in a family governed by the principles of reward and punishment with very little unconditional affirmation. The classic "firstborn" child, I was raised to be responsible and perform in order to obtain my parents' approval. When I first met Diana I was soon attracted to her in part because she did not seem very interested in my academic accomplishments. I was intrigued by the possibility that she saw something deeper within me that she valued. However, since we have been married, I tend to approach her seeming lack of interest in my career accomplishments in the light of my childhood need for my parents' approval. I seek her affirmation of my successes, just as I sought that affirmation from my parents. When she refuses to be drawn into that way of relating to me, I become wounded and can be reduced to adolescent pouting. Our marriage becomes salvific for me when I am able to recognize in these situations a call to go beyond the patterns of relating I brought into our marriage from my family of origin. To put the matter bluntly, my relationship with Diana demands that I grow up!

Marriage as Covenant

Christianity holds that what is unique about Christian marriage is the view that marriage is not merely a social contract between two people but a covenantal commitment that is grounded in God's covenantal commitment to Israel and Christ's covenantal commitment to the church. When Catholics speak of a marriage as a sacrament, they are drawing, in fact, on this covenantal perspective.

In the Hebrew scriptures there is no developed theology of marriage. However, what we do have is the use of the marriage relationship as a metaphor for God's covenantal relationship with Israel. This is developed in the book of Hosea, in which the story of faithful Hosea's pursuit of Gomer, in spite of her harlotry, is employed to exemplify God's fidelity with Israel. The covenant suggests God's unconditional commitment to Israel. I think it is difficult for us today to grasp the significance of this view of covenant because we live in a society so dominated by legal, contractual conceptions. In an oft-quoted article on Christian marriage, theologian Paul Palmer contrasts the notion of "contract" with that of "covenant":

> Contracts deal with things, covenants with people. Contracts engage the services of people; covenants engage persons. Contracts are made for a stipulated period of time; covenants are forever. Contracts can be broken, with material loss to the contracting parties; covenants cannot be broken, but if violated, they result in personal loss and broken hearts. Contracts are secular affairs and

belong to the market place; covenants are sacral affairs and belong to the hearth, the temple, or the church. Contracts are best understood by lawyers, civil and ecclesiastical; covenants are appreciated better by poets and theologians. Contracts are witnessed by people with the state as guarantor; covenants are witnessed by God with God as guarantor. Contracts can be made by children who know the value of a penny; covenants can be made only by adults who are mentally, emotionally, and spiritually mature.[27]

Covenant is ultimately about self-gift and involves a commitment of my very self to another person at the core of my being. Marriage is such an ancient and widespread social institution that we are inclined to miss how radical this notion of marriage is.

Imagine that you go to a car dealership to purchase a car. You find the car you are looking for and meet with the business manager to sign the papers. Everything is going smoothly until you come to the final page of the paperwork. It is a document that gives the dealer permission to come to your house at any point over the period that you own the vehicle and replace the car with a year, make, and model car of the dealer's choice. It could be a substantial upgrade or a substantial downgrade, and you will have no say in the decision. Who would buy a car with that degree of uncertainty?

Yet that is something of the kind of commitment that we enter into when we covenant to marry another person. It is easy to forget this when I promise myself to my beloved in the wedding ceremony. I may believe that I am promising myself to the woman standing opposite me. Such a promise seems quite reasonable and well grounded. I know this woman well. We have talked for hours together on every conceivable topic. A commitment to her seems a reasonable decision. It is on the basis of exactly this kind of judgment that so many foolishly enter the marital "house of mirrors" where nothing is as we thought it would be. The truth of the matter is that in a truly covenantal marriage I am also promising myself to the unknown person that my spouse will become in the future. I cannot possibly know who this person will be and yet, we Christians hold, our covenant promises fidelity to that unknown person of the future as well.

Here is where Christian faith and therapeutic insight come together. We hold that when we are faithful to the covenant of marriage and embrace this person to whom we have promised ourselves as the mysterious key to our salvation, God's grace is able to do its work in us. It is perhaps unavoidable that my description of this process of conversion in marriage will appear rather stark and negative. But this would be misleading, for it is also true that when we freely choose to live within the confines of a commitment made to this one person in covenantal love, there is a wonderful kind of liberation. We are liberated from the illusory fantasies of hypothetical relationships and unrealized choices to embrace the blessings of a real relationship with another flawed human being.

This insight is at the heart of the hilarious yet insightful novel by Nick Hornby, *High Fidelity*.[28] The novel offers a kind of male confessional that recounts the humorous story of a music "geek," Rob, who is in his midthirties, single, and owns his own record store. Along with his motley group of co-workers, Rob eats, drinks, and breathes pop music. They spend much of their time coming up with idiosyncratic top five lists (e.g., top five songs about death) and in fact use pop songs as a way of making sense of their lives. As Rob tells his story, we are introduced to a narcissistic and self-absorbed young man incapable of acknowledging his own responsibility for the failed relationships of his past. His latest girlfriend, Laura, has just moved out, and he is bitter and defensive about the breakup.

It becomes evident, as the novel progresses, that he "has issues," as they say, regarding commitment. His highly charged fantasy life stands as an obvious obstacle to sustaining a meaningful relationship. Not surprisingly, he fantasizes about having a relationship with a musician. He imagines her trying out new songs on him and making oblique references to him in the liner notes of her latest CD. However, when he is faced with the possibility of actually having an affair with a real musician, he becomes uneasy and is reluctant to proceed for fear that the real sexual encounter could not possibly live up to the thrill of the imagined *possibility* of such an encounter. He admits to the inevitable disillusionment he has experienced whenever he has cohabited with a woman because his romantic and even erotic fantasies of their life together could not be sustained. His difficulty with fantasies extends beyond the sexual arena. When Laura, his former girlfriend, confessed to him that she was not good at being real romantic and "slushy," he observed:

> That, to me, is a problem, as it would be to any male who heard Dusty Springfield singing "The Look of Love" at an impressionable age. That was what I thought it was going to be like when I was married. . . . I thought there was going to be this sexy woman with a sexy voice and lots of sexy eye makeup whose devotion to me shone from every pore. And there is such a thing as the look of love — Dusty didn't lead us up the gar-

den path entirely — it's just that the look of love isn't what I expected it to be. It's not huge eyes almost bursting with longing situated somewhere in the middle of a double bed with the covers turned over invitingly; it's just as likely to be the look of benevolent indulgence that a mother gives a toddler or a look of amused exasperation, even a look of pained concern. But the Dusty Springfield look of love? Forget it.[29]

This moment of recognition signals the beginning of Rob's maturation as he gets used to the idea that "my little-boy notion of romance, of negliges [sic] and candlelit dinners at home and long, smoldering glances, had no basis in reality at all."[30]

The turning point comes when Laura's father dies and Rob is invited to the funeral. Even though they are estranged, he is moved by Laura's obvious pain at the loss of her father. "And at that moment I want to go to her and offer to become a different person, to remove all trace of what is me, as long as she will let me look after her and try to make her feel better." Rob acknowledges and, in a real sense, repents of his narcissistic preoccupations. Later that evening, she embraces him in gratitude, "and when she lets go of me I feel that I don't need to offer to become a different person: it has happened already."[31]

Rob's maturation faces a final test near the end of the novel. He develops a crush on a journalist for a music magazine who was interviewing him. They plan a future meeting, purportedly to continue the interview, but with obvious expectations of more. In anticipation of their next meeting he begins his typical fantasizing about the two of them. The nervousness and excitement, the first kiss, the first sexual encounter, and so on. "When I meet her I know there'll be an initial twinge of disappointment — *this* is what all that internal fuss was about? — and then I'll find something to get excited about again. . . . And between the second and third meeting a whole new set of myths will be born." But this time something different occurs. As he daydreams about their future relationship he suddenly realizes "that there's nothing left to actually, like *happen*. I've done it all, lived through the whole relationship in my head." Rob sees that real relationships require dying to this ridiculous fantasy world. He realizes that his reluctance to commit to Laura lies in the fact that he'll never again experience with her that flush of excitement present at the beginning of any new relationship. "I've been thinking with my guts since I was fourteen years old, and frankly speaking, between you and me, I have come to the conclusion that my guts have shit for brains."[32]

At the close of the novel Rob meets with Laura and actually proposes. Laura, wise to his notorious fear of commitment, is skeptical. She questions how he can make a decision like this so suddenly. Rob protests and offers her the fruit of his recent reflections on relationships: "Just because it's a relationship, and it's based on soppy stuff, it doesn't mean you can't make intellectual decisions about it. Sometimes you just have to, otherwise you'll never get anywhere."[33] Rob has discovered that moving from one fantasy to another is no substitute for the sublime virtues of a real relationship with a real person.

Doubtless, *High Fidelity* offers a narrative of the struggle to attain mature, committed relationship from the male perspective. Both Diana and other women friends tell me that while they have recognized Rob's attitudes in their own relationships with men, they do not find the issues he struggles with to be their own. While I believe that marriage demands conversion from both husbands and wives, I suspect that there may be some gender-related differences in the nature of the concrete demand for conversion that marriage places on us. Nevertheless, all of us, male and female, must come to terms in our own way with the challenges and perils of maintaining a committed relationship with another imperfect, broken person.

Conclusion

It is said so often today that it has become a truism, but it bears repeating in this context: love is work. Rainer Maria Rilke, the famous German poet, wrote the following in one of his letters to an aspiring young poet:

> People have ... oriented all their solutions toward the easy and toward the easiest side of the easy; but it is clear that we must hold to what is difficult; everything alive holds to it, everything in Nature grows and defends itself in its own way and is characteristically and spontaneously itself, seeks at all costs to be so and against all opposition.... To love is good, too: love being difficult. For one human being to love another: that is perhaps the most difficult of all our tasks, the ultimate, the last test and proof, the work for which all other work is but preparation. For this reason young people, who are beginners in everything, cannot yet know love: they have to learn it.... The demands which the difficult work of love makes upon our development are more than lifesize, and as beginners we are not up to them. But if we nevertheless hold out and take this love upon us as burden and apprenticeship, instead of losing ourselves

in all the light and frivolous play, behind which people have hidden from the most earnest earnestness of their existence — then a little progress and an alleviation will perhaps be perceptible to those who come long after us; that would be much.[34]

What I am proposing in this chapter is that the graciousness and sacramentality of married life is not limited to expressions of marital intimacy. In this free embrace of emptiness and loneliness, of the needs not met, of fantasies not fulfilled, we are called to love not only out of the fullness of marital intimacy, but out of the emptiness of marital solitude. As spouses we are apprenticed to one another in the life of love, or, as Nancy Mairs put it, our spirits are "schooled in wedlock."

God help us to change. To change ourselves and to change our world. To know the need for it. To deal with the pain of it. To feel the joy of it. To undertake the journey without understanding the destination. The art of gentle revolution. Amen.[35]

Questions for Reflection and Discussion

1. How have you experienced your marriage as a crucible in which God has been transforming you more and more into the image of Christ?

2. Have you experienced the dynamic that Augustus Napier describes, that is, that we tend to marry into a situation that allows us to reenact basic issues and conflicts from our family of origin? If so, how have you and your spouse dealt with this?

3. Does your experience confirm or deny modern con-
   sumerism's influence on contemporary marriage? In
   what ways do you see the notion of covenantal marriage
   as radically counter-cultural and therefore a "daring"
   undertaking?

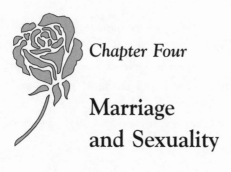

Chapter Four

Marriage
and Sexuality

In the adolescent fantasies of my generation (at least for us testosterone-charged males) the benefits of marriage began and ended with the prospects of sex without guilt. Indeed, it is surprising how much theological reflection on marriage still focuses on marital sex to the exclusion of the larger question of sexuality. In his younger years our present pope once wrote some rather provocative things about conjugal relations, offering perspectives that would have made his papal predecessors blush. Unafraid to discuss the sacramental significance of sexual union, the younger Karol Wojtyla even wrote of the value of married couples learning to achieve simultaneous orgasm![36] This is pretty racy stuff from a future pope, and knowing something of our church's dubious history in valuing sexual pleasure, I gratefully accept his view as a welcome corrective. I do worry, however, about a kind of romanticism in the Catholic tradition regarding marital sex.

I recall during my days in graduate school participating in a seminar on contemporary issues in moral theology. At the time we were reviewing Catholic church pronouncements on sexual ethics. One of the women in the seminar was an ordained Methodist minister, and at one point in our discussion she exclaimed in exasperation: "I don't get it with you Catholics! All of this talk of marital sex as the 'supreme expression of the marriage covenant' seems so much nonsense. When I think of those events that symbolically evoke the spiritual meaning of my marriage I think of my family at worship together receiving communion. For my husband and me, sex is more about joyful play than about making some symbolic gesture."

I am not yet ready to abandon the spiritual and even sacramental significance of conjugal relations — I do think we Catholics are on to something here — but as time goes on, I am inclined to believe that the distinctive blessing of sexual intimacy is more a gentle seal ratifying precious moments encountered outside the bedroom than the symbolic summit of marital love. In any event, it is impossible to consider conjugal relations apart from a larger reflection on human sexuality.

Genesis and the Gift of Sexuality

The book of Genesis boldly asserts that we are made in the image of God as male and female. That passage, with its familiar account of the creation of the world in six days, is contained in the first of two creation stories found at the beginning of Genesis. The significance of this assertion is explored in the second creation story. The main features of the story are familiar, but I would like to offer a provocative, new reading of this story suggested by the biblical scholar Phyllis Trible.[37] It begins as God scoops up the earth and breathes into it the breath of life, creating Adam, the first human. I have always assumed that "Adam" was a proper noun for the first human who was, of course, a male. It turns out, however, that "Adam" is not really a proper noun at all but simply the English transliteration for the Hebrew *ha adam* (only later in the story does it become a proper noun). *Ha adam* is itself a word-play on the Hebrew word for the earth, which is *ha adamah*. *Ha adam* means simply "a creature made from the earth." Moreover, there is nothing in the Hebrew to suggest that this creature yet possesses any gender, male or female. The first phase of this creation story begins, then, with a sexually indeterminate, solitary human.

God then creates various creatures, and brings them to Adam, this creature-made-from-the-earth, who names each animal, thereby demonstrating its dominance over the animal. Adam's needs for companionship having gone unmet, God puts the "earth creature" to sleep. The result of this divine surgery is not one new creature but two. First the woman, but also a transformed Adam who, in speaking for the first time, now refers to his new partner as *ishah*, "woman," and himself as *ish*, "man." Thus it is through the gift of sexuality that humanity finds its fulfillment. Prior to receiving the gift of sexuality, the first "human" was incapable of authentic fulfillment. Its only relationships were characterized by domination and therefore could not satisfy. Sexuality, experienced as a drivenness toward the other whom we recognize as our equal, becomes the means for our fulfillment. Our sexuality is the most profound signal we have that we are social beings; we are made for one another. Following Ronald Rolheiser, we might define sexuality as "a beautiful, good, extremely powerful, sacred energy, given us by God and experienced in every cell of our being as an irrepressible urge to overcome our incompleteness, to move toward unity and consummation with that which is beyond us."[38]

As the story continues another important fact is revealed. As the first man and woman looked upon one another, they were "naked" and they were not ashamed. In the Hebrew scriptures "nakedness" was generally a metaphor for both innocence and vulnerability. Frankly, the older I get, the more sense this makes. As my body's center of gravity begins its inexorable move "southward," the more I can appreciate nakedness as a metaphor for vulnerability. The nakedness of the first humans suggests that, prior to sin, man and woman were able to be naturally vulnerable, that is, transparent and powerless with one another. Grounded in trust and fidelity, the first humans could be confident that the power of sexuality inherent in being vulnerable before another would not be abused. They could risk disclosing themselves to the other without reserve, without deception. Unfortunately for humankind, the biblical story does not end with this paradisiacal state of confident vulnerability.

The story continues. The first humans are tempted by the serpent to partake of the fruit of the tree of the knowledge of good and evil with the promise that they shall become like God. And so it begins. The heart of human sin lies in the choice to be like God, not by grace as God intended, but by seeking complete autonomy and exercising absolute power and control over our lives. As the story progresses we learn that as a consequence of this primal sin the first humans become aware of their nakedness and quickly hide and clothe themselves. Once we humans make an option for absolute autonomy and control of our lives, the kind of interpersonal vulnerability that "nakedness" connotes becomes too risky. One of the regrettable consequences of original sin is that vulnerability no longer comes naturally. Rather than risk the possibility of pain and rejection that comes with vulnerability, we clothe ourselves with various "masks" and "fronts" that conceal our truest selves out of fear that who we really are will not be accepted by the other. We preen and strut, we blush coyly and adopt a thousand and one poses with studied intent. This emotional and psychological "clothing" becomes a means of manipulation. Sexual gamesmanship begins.

Sexuality vs. Genitality

This broken human condition presents the real challenge of marital sexuality. While magazine covers at the supermarket checkout lines trumpet "Ten Ways to Bring Your Lover to Ecstasy," the truth is that sexual technique is the least problematic aspect of sexuality. The real challenge that sexuality presents to us, a challenge as real for vowed celibates and single people as for married couples, is how to develop appropriately vulnerable relationships with others.[39] This is why it is so important to distinguish sexuality from genitality. Genitality addresses that complex set of behaviors, feelings, and dispositions associated with sexual intercourse and, as such, is but one dimension of human sexuality.

One of the real tragedies of the Catholic Christian tradition lies in the way that it consistently contrasted marriage and consecrated celibacy. Marriage was necessary for procreation and as an accommodation to human weakness (a "remedy to concupiscence") while consecrated celibacy constituted the "narrower way," the way of the spiritual hero or religious virtuoso. This tradition missed the opportunity to view marriage, vowed celibacy, and the single life as complementary witnesses to the life-giving power of human sexuality. The married couple's expression of their sexuality through "lovemaking" manifests to a world obsessed with the pornographic genitalization of sex that there is a huge difference between "having sex" and "making love." Married couples witness the possibilities for genital sex as a vital expression of intimacy and vulnerability made safe by their unconditional commitment to one another. At the same time, both vowed celibates and single persons witness an equally indispensable truth — that healthy sexuality and appropriate vulnerability is much more than genital sex and can be achieved without genital sex.

I do not mean to diminish the unique opportunities for intimacy and vulnerability that sexual intercourse offers married couples. It is undeniable that for married couples, genital sexual relations constitute a unique expression of our longing for intimacy. But here too the uniqueness and power of genital sex derives in large part from the vulnerability that such activity entails. Unlike numerous species in the animal kingdom, we humans make love to one another "face-to-face." The interpersonal intimacy that this profound human action involves is difficult to ignore. Indeed, the developed art of seduction and sexual gamesmanship was doubtless introduced as a means of avoiding the threat that intimacy at such close quarters presents. Herein lies the deep wisdom of Christianity in affirming marriage as the most adequate relational context for sexual intercourse. The danger of participating in genital sex outside of marriage lies not so much in the violation of a social taboo or the transgression of a divine command, but in the undeniable truth that genital sex exposes the participants to a level of interpersonal vulnerability fraught with risk. When one engages in this level of personal self-disclosure in a relationship not made safe by the bonds of trust that a lifelong, unconditional commitment to one another can bring, there can be serious harm. Perhaps traditional Christian sexual ethics has focused too much on sex as a kind of "marital privilege" and premarital sex as the

violation of a divine mandate. By focusing on the root issue
of appropriate vulnerability, we discover a new foundation for
sexual ethics:

> Any exercise of sexuality that violates appropriate vul-
> nerability is wrong. This includes violations of the
> partner's vulnerability and violations of one's own vul-
> nerability. Rape is wrong not only because it violates the
> vulnerability of the one raped, but also because the rapist
> guards his own power and refuses to be vulnerable. Sim-
> ilarly, seduction is wrong, for the seducer guards her or
> his own vulnerability and uses sex as a weapon to gain
> power over another. Any sexual encounter that hurts
> another, so that she or he either guards against vul-
> nerability in the future or is unduly vulnerable in the
> future, violates the "appropriate vulnerability" which is
> part of the true meaning and purpose of our God-given
> sexuality.[40]

This stress on "appropriate vulnerability" brings us back to
a central theme of this book, namely, that marriage is an
invitation to a privileged form of the life of communion.
Appropriate vulnerability can be thought of as a necessary
prerequisite for that communion. Unless I risk a certain degree of personal honesty in my relationship with my spouse,
there can be no authentic communion and, consequently, no
life of grace.

The Erotic Power of Marital Sexuality

The role of sexual intercourse in a marriage relationship can
change dramatically over the years. Early in a marriage it
is shot through with the eroticism and romance associated

with interpersonal discovery. The highly charged eroticism and passion of sex in a marriage is not without its spiritual significance. The compilers of the Hebrew scriptures adopted what was originally an erotic love poem, the Song of Songs, because they saw in the experience of human eroticism and passion a profound intimation of God's passionate, driven love for God's people.

> Ah you are beautiful, my beloved,
> ah, you are beautiful!
> your eyes are doves
> behind your veil ...
> your lips are like a scarlet strand;
> your mouth is lovely. ...
> Your breasts are like twin fawns,
> the young of a gazelle
> that browse among the lilies.
> (Song of Songs 4:1a, 3a, 5)

The implications are provocative. The inclusion of such poetry in the canon of the Bible invites the conclusion that the experience of passion and delight for one's beloved can itself be a participation in the love of God. This is a lot to take in. Most Catholic couples can handle, at least in theory, the sacramental significance of their coupling as a sign of the unity of Christ and his church. But it takes quite a leap to hold that the sharing of pleasure itself, the pure erotic energy between two people and their carnal delight in each other's bodies, is itself a communion in grace. Luke Timothy Johnson offers this perceptive observation:

> Many of us have experienced sexual passion as both
> humbling and liberating, a way in which our bodies know

quicker and better than our minds, choose better and
faster than our reluctant wills, even get us to where God
apparently wants us in a way our minds never could.[41]

Regrettably, today the "erotic" is more often associated with
the pornographic, or at best a "guilty pleasure," and is understood in a negative way. But this is not the root meaning of
eros.[42] *Eros* names the way in which we humans experience
desire as embodied spirits. It is associated with sensual pleasure and with self-gratification and is closely related to human
play. This in itself is an important insight. If we affirm that
making love can be a profound and solemn symbol of Christ's
love for the church, we must also affirm that making love can
be just as important as a medium of play and an occasion for
humor. Sex can be for many couples (and ought to be for all?)
an opportunity, in an atmosphere of covenantal trust, to risk
a liberating "silliness" so often repressed in the other, more
dignified spheres of our lives.

Eros means being aware that there is a playfulness that
ought to be associated with being embodied; it involves a delight for oneself and another. Our experience of the erotic
dimension of our existence is one of the most basic ways in
which we express self-love, but it is a uniquely relational self-
love. That is, in the experience of *eros* I experience self-love in
my desire for another. Desiring you brings delight to me. I desire the other, but my desire for the other is inseparable from
my own desire for self-gratification. I long for my beloved precisely because the very presence of my beloved is pleasurable
for me.

This experience of *eros* is often met with suspicion precisely
because of the pleasure-seeking that is implied. Christians
raised on the priority of divine love as *agape* are inclined to

think that the only love that deserves the name is that which is utterly self-less. Any act of love that is intermingled with pleasure and delight is thought to be a lower form of love. The roots of such a mistaken view are ancient. St. Augustine apparently held that before the Fall sexual relations lacked any significant experience of erotic pleasure; it was a biological act like any other. Only with the Fall and sin did erotic pleasure come to be associated with sex. We Christians have been struggling to recover a spiritual sense of sexual pleasure ever since.

It is a shame that the Christian tradition was not more influenced on this topic by another significant theologian in our tradition, Thomas Aquinas, for his views on the matter were quite different. Aquinas was convinced that before the Fall sexual relations between the first humans were *more* pleasurable than after the Fall.[43] The argument was simple: Before the Fall it would have been possible to enjoy bodily pleasures in due proportion without becoming obsessed with them. Sexual pleasure, experienced in a relationship where vulnerability comes naturally and without fear of hurt or betrayal, a relationship in which one delights in the other without turning the other into an object for gratification, is bound to be more pleasurable because it will be more *human.*

For Thomas the task of the human was not to become "pure," placing oneself above all earthly pleasures, but to become chaste, an altogether different matter. *Chastity* meant not a rejection of sexual desire, but a reintegration of sexual desire so that it shared fully in the meaning of human love. The chaste person exercised his or her "sexual appetite" (a technical scholastic term) in a manner that served or expressed human love. Thus for Aquinas, sexual pleasure was not at all evil or tainted by sin. As he put it, in words remarkable for their theological import if not for their romantic phrasing: "the abundance of pleasure in a well-ordered sex-act is not inimical to right reason."[44] His point was that sexual pleasure was a good and healthy thing as long as it was realized in actions intended not for pleasure alone but to serve the life of love.

The late moral theologian Andre Guindon used the analogy of music.[45] If we believe that all of us are born with a certain raw affinity for music, nevertheless it is true that this raw affinity must be cultivated. A trained music aficionado will have more cultivated tastes and be better able to discriminate between good and bad music. As audacious as it sounds, Thomas's theology would suggest that where sexuality is concerned, our spiritual task is not to overcome our sexual appetite nor to brutally master it, but rather to cultivate it in such a way that we become "sexual virtuosos." This should not be understood according to the model of Hugh Hefner. The goal is to become a person able to recognize the appropriate expression of sexual desire in a fully human context.

What is the difference, then, between, authentic erotic desire and that sin Christians have traditionally spoken of as "lust"? The answer is simple. Lust seeks no more than the gratification of a biological drive. When I am moved by lust the other person is completely incidental to my satisfaction. In true *eros* the other is desired for self-gratification but without a diminishment of the other. The erotic holds together "other-love" and "self-love" in a powerful, creative tension.

Sexual Passion and Human Compassion

Let me add a further dimension to the importance of erotic sexual passion and its attendant vulnerabilities. Consider the word "passion" itself. We often use it in reference to a deep longing or desire as when we speak, somewhat trivially, of "a passion for chocolate" or, more profoundly, of a "passion for justice." In this usage "passion" connotes a sense of life and vitality. Our use of the word in connection with sexuality and the erotic (e.g., "passionate lovemaking," "the throes of passion") is closely tied to this sense of desire or longing. This "passion" also suggests a certain vulnerability, for when we allow ourselves to experience longing there is always the possibility that we will not be satiated. In short, we risk failure. This may explain the application of "passion" to sexuality, for sexuality is one of the most powerful experiences of both human desire and human vulnerability.

Now let us consider a second meaning of the word "passion," seemingly at odds with the first. This meaning is usually rooted in a sense of suffering. In the Christian tradition we speak of the "passion of Jesus Christ." Here passion derives from its root in the late Latin usage of *passio*, which in turn was a translation of the Greek *pathos*. Yet this kind of "passion" also entails a sense of vulnerability — a willingness to undergo pain and loss. The only way to avoid suffering is to cease to feel, to anesthetize oneself. After all, it is from *pathos* that we get the Greek word *apatheia*, "apathy" in English, which is literally the absence of feeling or suffering. Apathy is, in some sense, a lack of passion.

Apathy, or the lack of passion, is a peculiarly modern problem. Apathy is present wherever in our culture there are people so obsessed with avoiding inconvenience, pain, or rejection that they end up avoiding all human relationships that require risk and vulnerability. It is an attitude that has become almost institutionalized in our society. We cede to professionals ancient familial responsibilities: care for those

who are emotionally wounded (the therapeutic professions),
care for the dying (professional nurses), care for the preparation of our deceased loved ones for burial (funeral directors
and morticians). We are tempted to quarantine ourselves from
all contact with pain, suffering, and death. Yet to live passionately is to embrace contact. It is to allow ourselves to
be vulnerable and be drawn into both our own and others'
delight and pain.

I contend that our capacity as married people to enjoy lusty
sexual passion (so far removed from its lust*ful* counterfeit in
promiscuous sexual congress) and the cultivated vulnerability
that such true sexual passion requires, may also help us to
cultivate an openness to real suffering and a compassion for
others. Provocative as it sounds, a vital, passionate sex life in
marriage may well school us in the ways of com-passion and
care for others.

...And Then Came the Children

The power of *eros* remains integral to marriage throughout the
life of the relationship. However, as a couple grows in their
marriage, their sexual relationship will often undergo significant changes as well. These changes come with increased
familiarity and as a result of any of a number of other factors,
the most dramatic of which is the introduction of children
into one's marriage. Indeed, I suspect that no single factor
has as decisive an impact on a couple's sexual life as children.
With the welcoming of children into the home there is a natural redirection of energy and attention from one's spouse
to the children. By the time dinner has been prepared and
consumed, dishes washed, children bathed, homework super-
vised, stories read, and children safely tucked into bed, the

possibilities for sexual intimacy fade in the face of nightly exhaustion. Spontaneous, playful "trysts" become less likely, and many couples struggle with what it means to have to "book" time for marital intimacy. For many there is a fear that the loss of spontaneity is a sign of some deeper problem in the marriage. It is easy to become convinced that other couples are having a lot more sex than we are!

Yet changes in both the frequency and "passion" of marital lovemaking need not be greeted with a sense of foreboding. It is often a sign of maturation in the marriage that lovemaking becomes both less frequent and less feverish. The patterns of lovemaking typical of early marriage can give way to a more occasional, warm, and tender experience that becomes in its own way even more satisfying than the sexual "wrestling matches" of our youth. At the same time, there may be a temptation to rationalize away the gradual disappearance of sexual intimacy in a marital relationship, avoiding the uncomfortable truth that this disappearance may be a harbinger of deeper problems in the marriage. While it is natural for couples to make love less frequently over time, and sustained sexual abstinence may be required for medical or other pressing reasons, sexual intimacy remains one of the most profound ways in which couples renew their commitment to one another. Given the frenetic pace of modern family life, unless couples make a conscious commitment to preserve times for sexual intimacy, this is often the likeliest aspect of marital life to be quietly abandoned.

I remarked earlier that there was a danger in much contemporary literature on Christian marriage to overly romanticize the spiritual significance of marital sex. I believe this to be true, but I also believe that the spiritual significance of marital lovemaking should not be discounted entirely. The physical and emotional vulnerability that making love evokes renders it a singularly powerful way for a couple to revitalize their marriage covenant as a commitment to be present to and for one another. It is not that this lovemaking is some privileged source of grace distinct from the many other forms of marital interaction. Married couples abide in God's love, whatever the circumstance, when they attend to one another in selfless devotion, placing the other's concerns before their own. But there is a sense in which a couple's sexual lovemaking ritualizes, as it were, the grace of their daily communion with one another. Just as the sacrament of reconciliation as celebrated in Roman Catholicism, for example, renders visible and effective that divine forgiveness that is always available to those who seek it, so marital lovemaking expresses or enacts in a particularly explicit way the grace of marital intimacy they share in their myriad daily encounters with each other. Mitch Finley puts it well:

> Shared sexual pleasure is central to a marital spirituality. Loving sexual intercourse is not just the icing on the cake for a healthy Catholic marriage. It is the cup God freely offers couples to nourish marital intimacy. ...Making love is basic to a couple's relationship with one another and with God. Regular, loving sexual intercourse is as fundamental to a marital spirituality as prayer is to the Christian life in general. Because love of God and neighbor cannot be divided, when husband and wife cultivate intimacy with one another, they also nurture their intimacy with God. To put this another way, the bodily way husband and wife nourish their love is also the most spiritual way.[46]

Mary Anne McPherson Oliver has sketched out a "conjugal spirituality" that requires that married couples appropriate the spiritual disciplines necessary for them to thrive. Whereas the primary spiritual disciplines of monastic life were those of fasting, solitary prayer, communal prayer, *lectio divina* (the practice of reading aloud the scriptures or some other sacred text), and common labor, marriage possesses its own unique spiritual disciplines. The two spiritual disciplines she provocatively highlights are talk and sex.[47] By "talk" she means the conjugal discipline of meaningful conversation, which in turn requires the cultivation of the skills of "listening, empathizing, confronting," and diplomacy in the face of conflict. By "sex" she means "that extraordinarily powerful uprising which can tear us out of ourselves, carry us beyond our mind and senses, and at its departure leave our heightened consciousness at peace and naturally open to a changed world."[48] While conjugal relations between husband and wife do not necessarily represent the pinnacle of sacramental marriage, making love is part of the spiritual discipline of married life, a discipline that is by turns earnest and centering, playful and silly.

Procreation and Marital Generativity

The Eastern Orthodox tradition offers a quite distinctive approach to sacramental marriage. It views the married couple as a living icon of the Trinity. Consider that in the triune life of God the love between two (the Father and the Son) is not self-contained but "spills over," as it were, as Spirit. The triune life of God is characterized not only by a profound mutuality of love between the Trinitarian persons, but also by a fecundity, a superabundance in which God's love overflows outward into the world. The doctrine of the Trinity teaches us that authentic love can never be contained in the private commerce of two lovers. A love between two, sustained in the long term, is always inadequate and faces the dangers of fixation and egocentricity. A Trinitarian love is one that flows outward beyond the two. In marriage, as Trinitarian icon, this is fittingly expressed in childbearing as a concrete expression and extension of the couple's love. When a married couple brings children into the world, they are sharing profoundly in the creative purposes of God.

The generative dimension of marriage is also reflected in the married couple's call to mission, to expansive community. Consequently in Orthodoxy childbearing is not seen as an obligation of married life (as it often has been understood in certain Roman Catholic theologies of marriage) but as a "felicitous outcome" of the nuptial union.[49] The marriage relationship reveals the inadequacy of a community of two and thus differentiates itself from the often closed relationship of two romantic lovers.

Catholicism's traditional focus on *procreation* in marriage might be broadened profitably by consideration of the marital *generativity* suggested by this Trinitarian perspective. There are a number of reasons for preferring to focus on the larger generative dimension of the marriage relationship. First, and most obviously, not all married couples can have children. The Catholic Church's strong emphasis on the obligation to have children has left many infertile couples feeling as if they were defective, second-class participants in the sacrament of matrimony. Second, a married couple normally outlives their childbearing years. It is important that Christianity offer a spirituality for married couples that engages them across the entire lifespan of their marriage.

The positive insight of the Catholic tradition is rooted in the fact that bearing children is in truth a particularly profound and apt expression of this generativity. For most married couples the generative power of their love will indeed be expressed in childbearing and childrearing. I will want to reflect on this important dimension of married life in the next chapter. But generativity, the drive to see our love bear fruit in the world, can be expressed in innumerable ways. This is the aspect of Christian mission which is so strong in the Orthodox view of marriage and relatively undeveloped in most other Christian traditions. The love of husband and wife takes on a public dimension in marriage that impels them outward in service of the world. This shift is reflected in the transposition of postures that takes place in the wedding ritual itself. At the exchange of vows the couple faces each other, each entering into covenant with the other. Then, however, the couple is presented to the community, and they move from a posture in which they are facing each other to one in which side by side they are facing first the Christian community and, beyond it, the world at large.

For some couples the commitment to mission has meant a ministry of hospitality in which unwed mothers and the homeless are given a place to stay in an atmosphere of Christian love. Other couples have been foster parents or have served in soup kitchens or food pantries. Still others engage in formal ministries within the church or host faith sharing and Bible study groups. Whatever the case, these married couples are allowing their love to be fruitful in Christian service. A spirituality of marriage would be horribly defective if it did not recognize the generativity of marriage as a call to mission and service in the church and world. It is only from within this commitment to generativity that it is possible to consider a topic that has literally reshaped American Catholicism since Vatican II — artificial birth control.

The Challenge of Responsible Parenthood in a Technological Culture

One of the most important statements on marriage in the documents of the Second Vatican Council came in its Pastoral Constitution on the Church in the Modern World. In that document the council offered a theological vision of marriage that went far beyond the largely contractual notion that had dominated Catholic church teaching prior to the council. The bishops wrote of marriage as an "intimate partnership of life and love" (no. 48). They affirmed that married love is, in its own way, a participation in divine love. They described conjugal love as expressing two dimensions, the unitive and the procreative, without, however, suggesting that the procreative had priority over the unitive, as had earlier church pronouncements. The council spoke as well of the need for parents to act responsibly in their decisions to bring children into the world as both "cooperators" with and "interpreters" of God's love. This will demand considerable discernment, taking into account both their own welfare and that of their children (no. 50). Then the council warned vaguely against using illicit forms of birth regulation. The council addressed this matter in very general terms because Pope Paul VI had promised to set up a special commission to consider the question after the close of the council.

That commission, comprised of bishops, theologians, and lay persons, overwhelmingly recommended to Pope Paul VI that church teaching be revised to permit, in exceptional situations, recourse to artificial forms of birth regulation. A minority report was also issued by some members of the commission; it rejected this recommendation, concerned that a change in church teaching would undermine the credibility of the church's teaching office. In 1968, in the midst of a broad expectation of change in the church's position, Pope Paul VI issued his controversial encyclical *Humanae vitae,* in which he reaffirmed the church's traditional opposition to artificial birth control. His argument was that the conjugal act was intrinsically ordered to the transmission of life even when conception could not be realized either because a couple was having sexual relations during an infertile period in the woman's reproductive cycle or because of general infertility. Consequently any artificial intrusion into the sexual act that would render the act "infecund" would be immoral because it would wrongly separate the unitive from the procreative dimension of the conjugal act. At the same time, the pope did approve certain "natural" methods (often referred to as "natural family planning") that would allow a couple to determine when the woman was ovulating and then to abstain from sexual relations during those periods (changes in a woman's body temperature and the viscosity of vaginal mucous can help a couple detect when the woman is ovulating).[50]

In the thirty plus years since the encyclical, the pope's teaching has been roundly criticized by many theologians, cautiously avoided by many clerics, and widely ignored by a considerable majority of the laity. What are we to make of this situation?

First, it must be noted that the teaching of Pope Paul VI has not been one of those embarrassing pronouncements furtively swept under the carpet, not to be discussed in respectable company. Pope John Paul II has reasserted this teaching without either hesitation or equivocation. Indeed, he has given the teaching a new impetus by linking it to his sweeping condemnation of the "culture of death" rampant in modern civilization. The new context in which this teaching has been placed merits serious consideration. We live in an age, the pope has often reminded us, in which our technological ingenuity has allowed us to conquer disease and improve the quality of life of millions. At the same time it has created the myth of human domination and control. We have come to view any and all constraints on our freedom as something to be conquered. Technology has been the weapon we have wielded, to great effect, in our battle to gain complete mastery over our world and over time itself. We have become enamored with the ways in which technological gadgetry can free us from the burdens of our daily engagements and allow us to excise the wasted time in our lives previously spent laboring over the trivial.[51] We live in a culture that champions efficiency and convenience as the highest values.

But in such a technological world, what has become of the grace of waiting, the anticipation of the unknown and unplanned, the openness to surprise? Is there not a danger that our preoccupation with efficiency and convenience has led us to cheapen and even ignore altogether the distinctive blessings that come as we embrace the necessity of certain constraints. Perhaps the matter can be seen in a fresh light if we look to the way we use technology, not so much to prevent conception, as to plan for the birth of a child.

My wife and I have had four pregnancies. One ended in miscarriage, in two other pregnancies the onset of labor was artificially induced, and yet another occurred "naturally," which is to say, according to the child's schedule and not ours. The difference in the experiences was striking. The miscarriage itself was a painful experience of the fragility of life and a sobering realization that we Catholics, for all of our convictions about the sanctity of life from conception on, have a long way to go in learning to attend pastorally to those who suffer the pain of miscarriage.

The experience of waiting for the "natural" onset of labor was unique. We knew the baby could come at any time over the period of almost a month. With every pain Diana experienced we wondered, "Was this it?" And then came the frenetic activity when the labor actually began — calling family and friends, getting the car packed.

By contrast, the two cases in which the labor was artificially induced were far less tense. We had an appointment at the hospital and so knew several days in advance when the labor would begin. It certainly allowed us to prepare for the event and minimize possible schedule conflicts. Yet what made the pregnancy ending in the natural onset of labor so different from those that ended with an artificial induction was precisely that the former was beyond our control. The baby was going to come according to his schedule, not ours. Waiting for the labor to begin was a profound lesson in abandonment, giving up control of our lives. That is why I think it so telling that today a far greater number of pregnancies end with labor artificially induced than was the case twenty years ago. Of course many of these are for medical reasons, but more and more are not. I raise this concern with the honest admission that we too induced labor on one occasion for nonmedical reasons.

The experience has led us to reflect more on what is lost in the experience of an artificially induced labor. When scheduling a birth around vacations and business trips is as easy as the scheduling of dental appointments, is there a danger of diminishing the sanctity of the birth itself? Are we losing one of the precious gifts that a pregnancy offers us — namely, the wonderful blessings that come when we become receptive to that which is beyond our control? The hard truth is that we cannot plan for or manipulate God's grace. Our lives are blessed to the degree that we are receptive to the moment as parents who must be open and ready for the onset of labor.

Seen from this perspective there is much to commend in the insistent teaching of both Pope Paul VI and Pope John Paul II on the dangers of artificial birth regulation. They remind us that we live in a culture governed by a convenience mentality in which artificial birth control can easily become simply another way in which we seek to master the world around us, including the gift of life. They warn of the real danger that human life itself could soon become a commodity like the laptop computer we can special order on the Internet, made to our precise needs and specifications.

We should also remember that papal teaching does not condemn all means of birth regulation. Natural family planning (NFP) honors the need for parents to fulfill their vocation to bring children into the world with due responsibility. Natural Family Planning has much to commend it. It is a method that allows the couple to work in harmony with the woman's natural reproductive cycle rather than relying on intrusive artificial methods, many of which may do harm to a woman's health. NFP also requires communication and cooperation between the husband and wife, rather than foisting responsibility on one of the parties to take a pill or use a condom. While the method does require periodic abstinence each month, these periods can provide opportunities for the couple to explore other ways of expressing their love for one another.

For all of these reasons, it is regrettable that the teaching of Pope Paul VI has been simply ignored by millions of Catholics. However, not everyone who disagrees with the papal teaching has simply ignored it. For while there is an undeniable wisdom in recent papal teaching, many thoughtful Catholics, including some bishops and Catholic theologians, have wondered whether an absolute prohibition of artificial birth control can really be sustained. These voices are too many to simply be dismissed as faithless and disobedient malcontents. The concerns they raise are real. They note that while Pope Paul VI speaks of the nature of the "conjugal act," that conjugal act is always engaged in by persons, and those persons to a large extent invest their actions with meaning by way of their intentions. The physical act that takes place in a rape is the same as the physical act in which a husband and wife ratify their love for one another. It is the different *intentions* and the different contexts that give decisively different meanings to the two respective sex acts. It is simply insufficient to speak of the nature of the act itself apart from a consideration of the relationship in which the act takes place.

Papal teaching is certainly prophetic in its condemnation of the "contraceptive mentality" dominant in our culture in which convenience becomes the paramount value in decisions about parenthood. At the same time, some ask whether it is possible for a couple to be truly open to new life in the context of their whole marital relationship without each individual sex act having to be "open" to new life. These dissenting voices argue that there are extraordinary circumstances in which couples, because of financial constraints or personal limitations, simply cannot fulfill their parental obligations responsibly and have more children. It is not a question of a lack of heroism, but of a heightened sense of moral obligation to care for the children they already have and nurture their marriage.

Is it not possible, however, to honor obligations to responsible parenthood by using NFP? In many instances these methods do work well, but it is simply disingenuous to present NFP as the panacea for responsible parenthood in all situations, as Mitch Finley has noted.[52] In spite of protests by proponents of NFP, the method does present some difficulties. The most significant is that the method depends on periodic abstinence. Now this can have undeniable benefits for couples who can use the time of abstinence as an occasion for discovering other ways to express their love. However, the period of abstinence, if one includes the period when a woman is menstruating (a time when many couples prefer to abstain from sexual relations anyway), can range from eleven to sixteen days in a monthly reproductive cycle. This is a significant period of time for many couples who, if they have children, are often struggling as it is to keep sexual intimacy alive in their marriage. Factor in the circumstances in which one or the other of the spouses has a job requiring travel for extended periods of time and the demands of periodic abstinence can be transformed from "an opportunity to find other ways to express their love" into a major obstacle in the marriage relationship.

So where does all of this leave us? For Roman Catholics, the teaching of *Humanae vitae* is authoritative and cannot be dismissed or ignored. Catholics must make a good faith effort to embrace the official teaching of the church, and they should insure that if they have difficulties with this teaching, these difficulties do not stem from either an inadequate understanding of the church's teaching or an unwillingness to live according to the often demanding norms of Christian life. In a culture obsessed with efficiency, convenience, and control, the latter is a very real possibility. Finally, it must be pointed out that while this teaching is authoritative, the majority of theologians do not believe it has been taught infallibly; there does exist the remote possibility of error, and Catholics who make a good faith effort to align themselves with this teaching but find they simply cannot discover in it God's will can and must follow their consciences in this matter. In any case, this teaching is a sober reminder that with the power to bring forth life comes a tremendous responsibility to form our marriage relationships in ways that stand as a ringing affirmation of the dignity of human life and the blessings that come with the vocation to parenthood.

Nowhere are the complexities of our humanity displayed more vividly than in the experience of human sexuality. As sexual beings we experience a deep longing for communion with one another. Yet as sexual beings we also discover that at a very deep level that longing can never be fulfilled completely by another human being, no matter how much that person is the object of our love and devotion. Our sexuality leads us to engage in selfless acts of love; when distorted, it can lead us to acts of selfishness and betrayal. Our sexuality can yield both our exaltation and our humiliation. In marriage, our sexuality draws us together and, on occasion, keeps us apart. It makes us capable of play, delight, and the risk of vulnerability. As sexual beings married couples ratify their covenantal love for one another in conjugal union. As sexual beings married couples welcome the possibility that the ratification of that covenantal love might yield new life. In the end, our sexuality holds out for us a tentative but real anticipation of our ultimate destiny with God, where play and delight, risk and self-sacrifice, fecundity and creativity all find their final consummation in eternal communion.

Questions for Reflection and Discussion

1. Does your own "sexual history" confirm the insight that the key to authentic sexuality is appropriate vulnerability?

2. How have you struggled with maintaining real vulnerability in your own marriage?

3. How comfortable are you with the idea that the erotic dimension of marital sexuality is good and sacred?

4. How have you experienced the power of generativity in your marriage? In what ways?

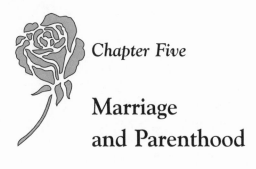

Chapter Five

Marriage and Parenthood

Certainly chief among marriage's blessings are the children. Diana and I are the parents of four young boys, and in part because of them our married life has taken on a mood and a texture that we could not have anticipated. In Catholic teaching there are three ministries within the one sacrament of Holy Orders (deacon, priest-presbyter, and bishop); there are times when I think the church would have done well to create two degrees of marriage: one with children and one without! Theoretically, the children are distinct from our marital relationship yet, upon appearing, they are often the most visible sign of what our union has come to be. Many of us married with children could secretly confess a dark and desperate time when it was the faces of our children that made us try harder to heal whatever rift threatened to become an unbridgeable chasm in our marriage.

I struggled over whether a book on marital spirituality ought to address the question of parenthood. Clearly, not all married couples are parents, and I do not want to suggest that their relationship is in any sense deficient because of this. Yet for those of us who are married and parents, it is impossible to separate completely the two roles. I recognize the distinction between my role as a husband and as a fa-

ther, but I cannot help seeing profound connections between
the two. I parent our children *as* Diana's husband — it is as
simple as that. Both relationships involve life-long commitments and demand firm spiritual foundations. Together these
two interlocking commitments to spouse and child provide
the privileged context in which I am being molded by God's
grace into something new.

I have no interest in offering guidelines here on the "how
to's" of good parenting. My interest runs in another direction. Instead I wish to explore how the role of parent informs
and deepens my role as spouse and vice versa, calling me
to growth, to change, to conversion. A fruitful starting point
may be the sense of marital companionship that we considered
earlier.

Marital Companionship and Parenting

Marital companionship, "sharing bread together," goes beyond
the ways in which husband and wife are called to nourish one
another. Marital companionship also includes the common
labor a couple undertakes together. This labor becomes for
them the "bread" they share with the world. In marriage a
new community is established (a domestic church) offering
the world the shared fruit of the couple's relationship. This is
why for many married couples their experience of marriage is
so closely tied to their children.

I feel fortunate to belong to that first modern generation
that considered it appropriate for the father to be present at
the birth of the child. Diana and I were never so profoundly
"companions" as when our twins, David and Andrew, were
born. One was placed gently on Diana's chest while I held the
other gingerly in my arms. A similar scene was enacted with

our two other children, Brian and Gregory. These children have become our "shared bread," our common work.

I have often been struck by this sense of parenting as a common labor in the presence of several mature married couples whose children have long since moved out of the home. One such couple, Winnie and Wally, would, over dinner, offer us tales of their own struggles raising four boys. As they shared with us their stories, chuckling and exchanging knowing glances throughout, they offered us, with disarming honesty, both their successes and their misgivings. As I recall those treasured meals, it seems to me now that their children were the "bread" they firmly kneaded and patiently baked in their home as an offering to God and world.

Later, long after their children had grown up and left home, they experienced their adult children in a new way when they returned to visit. Stories of these visits, told with the same love and affection, nevertheless were cast differently. The children were no longer living projects to be shaped by parental hands; they were now adults who had gone out into the world where, by turns, they stumbled and flourished. In any case, they returned home as individual adults with their own tales to be told, tales in which the influence of their parents appeared less significant. These adult children now represented "return gifts" to be welcomed and embraced by their parents. So it is that the bread we offer the world returns to us transformed for our delight and nourishment.

For most couples this marital dynamism of offering and return is experienced in the process of parenting. Yet another couple comes to mind, Sam and Nancy, who were not able to have children but worked for years to start a soup kitchen in their small town. Finally they were able to establish one, and within two years had forged relationships with many of the area churches. This common endeavor had become their shared bread. I know other couples whose children have grown and yet who share common labor in the way they welcome teenage unwed mothers into their home, where they can finish school while they have their baby. Here again we witness bread offered to the world, only to return in new and unexpected ways. Whenever a couple engages in common labor, in service of the church or the larger human community, they are true companions.

This profound movement in marriage in which common labor is offered and returns as gift is enacted liturgically in the Roman Catholic celebration of the eucharist. In the liturgy the gifts of bread and wine are set on a table in the back of the church and, at the appropriate moment, are brought forward by members of the assembly to be placed on the altar. The priest prays over these gifts a prayer that has its roots in the ancient Jewish liturgical tradition:

> Blessed are you Lord God of all creation, for through your goodness we have this bread to offer, which earth has given and human hands have made; it will become for us the bread of life.... Blessed are you Lord God of all creation, for through your goodness we have this wine to offer, fruit of the vine and work of human hands; it will become our spiritual drink.

The bread of the eucharist is not mere wheat; it is wheat transformed by human hands into bread. The wine is more than grapes, it is grapes transformed by human hands. These offerings are the fruit of human labor offered to God only to be returned as wondrous gift, "our spiritual food and drink."

This brief meditation on marital companionship suggests a way in which the married couple, as a domestic church, a church of the home, is also a eucharistic community. When I was growing up in the late 1960s and 1970s it was common for Catholic families to invite the parish priest into one's home to conduct a "home mass" for a small gathering of family and close friends. This celebration of the eucharist in the home was seen as a wonderful way to "sacralize" home life. However, what I am suggesting here is that when married couples live the life of communion as true companions, the fruit of their shared labor is already a form of "eucharist" in which "bread" is shared. Parenthood possesses an undeniably eucharistic character.

Let us now turn more directly to consider parenthood and the ways in which it provides the occasion for God to continue that good work begun in us.

The "Good" Parent

I have no illusions regarding my abilities as a parent. As a father I seem to commit parenting blunders at an almost alarming rate. Diana clearly has more of an instinct for this than I do. This is not to say that I am a bad parent; I am simply not an exemplary one. But then my personal standard for being a "good parent" has lowered substantially over the years. In the early years of my marriage, when children were still part of an uncertain future, "ideal parents" were ones who never raised their voice because they did not need to; they spoke with a quiet wisdom that virtually commanded respect. "Ideal parents" never laid a hand on their children, never employed hurtful sarcasm. "Ideal parents" always gave their children their undivided attention. "Ideal parents" patiently explained their actions, particularly as they affected their children.

Needless to say, my standards have changed, becoming considerably more modest. I have abandoned all hope of ever being the "ideal parent." I now aspire to be merely a "reasonably good parent," the chances of success being much improved. "Reasonably good parents" love their children even if they do not always show it. Good parents do communicate their love to their children in both words and gestures — even if these affectionate words and gestures are interspersed with other words and gestures that communicate anger and frustration. "Good parents" are present — perhaps not always emotionally attentive — but present. The child must know that though parents may become angry, may even take on the appearance of an apoplectic seizure, they will not leave them, not today, not ever. "Good parents" acknowledge the importance of the parental "rules of engagement," even if they do not always live up to them. These rules prohibit parenting by fear or taking advantage of the inherent inequity of power in the parent-child relationship. They prohibit a parent from taking out adult frustrations on the child. "Good parents" are likely to break these rules often, but then have the courage to admit it to their children. "Good parents" see to it that their children know that in their parents they have an emotional safety net under the terrifying highwire act of childhood and adolescence. Good parents strive to be coach, cheerleader, and team doctor all rolled into one.

I believe I pass this lower standard. Do I yell more than I would like? Yes. Do I discipline out of anger? Yes. Am I ashamed to say that I have acted in ways that at times have led my children to fear me? Yes. Do I ignore their needs and dismiss them when I should listen? Again, yes. So I am by no means an "ideal parent," but I am a "good" one, if only because I long to be one and am determined not to abandon this longing. It also means that I am humbled by my vocation and reminded daily by the faces of my children that there is much in me that has yet to yield to God's transforming grace. Those faces also remind me that my children are paying for this stubbornness.

Re-Visioning Parenthood

My years as a parent have led me to a certain "revisionist" thinking about the traditional understanding of the parental role. If an authentic spirituality of marriage is to incorporate the wisdom gleaned from parenting, conventional accounts of parenting may require some reworking. I have in mind here three actions I have always viewed as foundational to parenting: providing, protecting, and forgiving.

The Parent as Provider

As parents we have inherited deep-rooted expectations about being a provider to our children. This is not all to the bad. Many of us learned much from fathers and mothers who taught us the values of industry, responsibility, perseverance, and self-discipline necessary to support a family. At the same time, the stereotype of the parental provider carries with it some dangers. The indispensable responsibility to provide for a family, if we are not careful, can blind us to our need, not only to provide for our children, but to engage them in relationship. I speak freely of my children as "living sacraments," effective signs of God's love. But the hard truth is that they cannot be "sacrament" to me unless I am present to them. We live in a culture that sets up the expectation that we provide for our children at least as well, if not better, than our parents provided for us. In an ever more materialistic culture, provision for our children cannot help but be translated into material provision. It has become a reflex gesture within our culture to express our care in material terms. The best neighborhoods, the best schools, the best clothes, the best sports programs, all these things, we come to believe, are the concrete measure of our success as providers. It is a myth that often serves to justify long days at the office and the inexorable climb up the corporate ladder.

In truth there is nothing wrong with the view of the parent as provider. The difficulty is that we tend to become preoccupied with the wrong "provisions." Beyond the bare minimums of a home that protects our loved ones from the elements (meteorological and criminal), nutritious food on the table, serviceable clothes, and safe educational opportunities, our children's material needs are surprisingly few. The most compelling provision required by our children is parental presence and engagement, and, lamentably, this presence and engagement cannot be strictly scheduled.

Herein lies the difficulty with the notion of "quality time" with our children. For me an example of "quality time" would be the time I set aside to go to a Houston Astros game with my boys or to read with them at night before bed. This "quality time" is important. But there is a depth and a texture to my experience of my children that often doesn't emerge in such carefully planned events but rather in the "down time" when nothing important seems to be happening. An example would be the time, driving my youngest child home from preschool, when I listened to him making up a hymn with a spontaneous and hilarious mélange of disconnected religious images. It was a musical creation I would not have heard if I were on the cell phone taking care of business. Or the time when we were all in the kitchen making pizza and my two youngest boys, Brian and Gregory, each put pots on their heads and ran headlong into each other like two feuding billy goats crashing into each other, then falling down on the ground laughing hysterically. I am spectacularly unsuccessful in planning "quality" interaction with my children. Invariably, I will ask them some serious question about their hopes and dreams only to be met with a puzzled or even bored look on their faces. No, these interactions generally happen according to an inscrutable calendar in which I have no choice but to wait, being, first and crucially, available and attentive to that random moment when my child suddenly blurts out his greatest fear or proudly shares his greatest achievement.

The grace that comes to us in the lives of our children comes to us as surprise, often in the delightfully unexpected moments: while working on the lawn, preparing a family meal together, or running family errands. The notion of quality time with our children, a notion with origins in time management principles appropriate to the workplace, ignores the fact that quality interaction with our children cannot be programmed. Much of what I have come to know about the life of communion I first learned through my children. To live in communion is to be attentive, in the present moment, to the presence of the other. The life of communion, like quality time, cannot be "booked." The central provision I am called to offer my wife and children is, quite simply, me — fully present and open to discovering the marvelous gift that they are for me.

The Parent as Protector

Protecting my children is almost as fundamental to my conception of parenting as that of providing for them. Again, seeing oneself as a protector of children is not necessarily a

bad thing. It is a great gift to our children for both father
and mother to offer them a sense of protection and stability,
to reassure them that their home is indeed, both physically
and emotionally, a "safe" place. But to a greater extent than I
think most of us realize, our role as protector is illusory. This
was brought home to me painfully several years ago.

We were returning from a family vacation when we were
involved in a serious car accident on the interstate. There was
a pile up a half mile ahead, and in the process of braking I
lost control of our van, smashed sidewise into a truck pulling
a boat, and caromed through the grass median and directly
into oncoming traffic. When I finally regained control of the
van and pulled off onto the shoulder, I turned around to see
all four of our children crying, and one of them, Brian, bleed-
ing profusely from his head and face. The ambulance quickly
arrived and, because the paramedics feared he might have a
serious head or spinal injury, Brian was strapped to a gurney
and whisked off to the nearest emergency room. It turned out
that his injuries were not serious, and he, along with the rest
of the children and Diana, was fine. But forever etched in my
memory will be the sight of my four children screaming in fear
and pain. As the driver of the van, I felt responsible for what
happened. At a very deep level, I believed I had failed them.
I had broken some unspoken covenant — a silent agreement
ratified by countless acts of care — in which I promised that
I would protect them from harm. The experience has forced
me to reassess my parental identity as protector. It made me
realize that, in fact, I cannot really protect my children at all.
I cannot promise them that they will never be hurt or feel
pain, loss, or tragedy. There is no parental "force field" that I
can project around them to keep them secure.

This recognition has not come easily to a person like myself, because, while the desire to protect is good and noble, it often veils a deeper and more questionable desire to control the lives of others. This operates on two levels. On the first level is the pain I feel at the pain of my loved ones. I grew up as a child feeling very insecure as I was often the butt of jokes because of my nerd-like appearance and demeanor. In consequence, I find it excruciatingly painful to watch one of my children teased in a like fashion. A forty-three-year-old man with four college degrees, I can be reduced to the most juvenile of attitudes, "telling off" the perpetrators of my child's perceived injury as if the battles my children face were the laboratory in which I might finally resolve my own issues. Yet the letting go that is demanded here, allowing my children to deal with taunts and insults, is as difficult for me as it is necessary for them.

What I have learned about myself as parent also informs my role as a spouse. If it is true that I cannot protect my children from pain, it is even more true of my wife. I often find myself slipping into the role of parent/protector with her as well. I recall an instance in which Diana had a "falling out" with a friend. I made the fatal mistake of intervening on her behalf, only to make the situation considerably worse. I wish I could say that I learned from that mistake, but there are numerous other instances of my trying to intervene in outrage because of the pain that another person or persons may have caused my wife.

As a firstborn, I was affirmed at an early age as the family "fixer," the one who could intervene in troubled family situations and resolve the dispute. I have carried this "fixer" role into my marriage and family and am still struggling to admit that in many instances what I was trying to fix was my own discomfort and impotence in the face of the pain of someone I loved. Committed love leaves us open to that peculiar pain felt when we dare to "share the pain" of another without trying to make it go away. All I can promise my wife and my children is my attentiveness, my compassionate presence, my commitment never to abandon them in their pain. Indeed, this is all God promises any of us, and to embrace this as parent and spouse is to accept our own humble role as instruments of God's compassionate presence.

Abandoning the role of protector is an invitation to enter once more into the rhythm of the paschal mystery, dying to the presumption that I have or ought to have absolute control over the ultimate destiny of my wife and children. If I am honest with myself, there is a hubris in overestimating my impact on my children's still young lives — for they too are sturdily, resiliently *other*, a mystery unfolding that I may feel compelled to nudge along but can never wholly direct. I am invited to embrace their own developing life stories as *their* stories, stories that must be written through their choices as much as by my counsel, protection, and care.

Dispensing Mercy, Offering Forgiveness: Participating in the Household of God

The "good parent" forgives. I know few parents who would not think of themselves as forgiving. I always assumed I qualified. I have always felt confident that there is nothing my children could do that I would be unwilling or unable to forgive. Yet recent reflections on a well-known biblical story have led me to consider anew the true demands of parental forgiveness.

We all know the basic plot: a father has two sons, and the younger approaches the father and asks for his inheritance. This was a highly unusual and harsh request in ancient times for two reasons. First, to ask a father to divide his inheritance was essentially to rob him of a livelihood in his final years. Second, because such a gesture represented a dismissal of the father's value to the son, the younger son was essentially saying he could not wait for his father to die. In any event, the son then proceeds to "squander his inheritance." Soon he is hiring himself out to care for swine. So hungry is he that even the pig slop looks appealing. It is at this point that the biblical text introduces a detail that somehow I never really caught before. The son "comes to his senses" and realizes how much better off were the servants at his father's house. An idea comes to him: "I shall get up and go to my Father and *I shall say to him*, 'Father I have sinned against heaven and against you...'" (Luke 15:18).

Maybe it is because I now read the text as a father in a way that I never did before, but I am troubled by a question that will not go away: Is the son truly contrite or is he just hungry? Is the son merely plotting: "What words must I offer to regain my father's favor?" My suspicious, fatherly heart wonders whether he is seeking to regain admission into the household but without genuine repentance. I've seen this on the face of my own children: "What do I need to say to him that will keep me from being grounded?" The point is not minor because, while I can imagine nothing my children might do for which I would not extend forgiveness, I would expect a genuine expression of contrition as a prerequisite for that forgiveness. Yet such does not appear to be the case for the father in the parable. When he sees the son coming at a distance, he does not wait for a profession of contrition but rather, in an action most unseemly for a father of that time, runs to embrace him. It is only after this embrace that the son offers what is apparently an authentic confession of sin.

This parable goes far beyond the world of parental forgiveness that I know. Is Jesus really suggesting that in his Father's house this is how forgiveness works? Are we supposed to extend forgiveness even prior to an expression of authentic repentance? This text shines an uncomfortably harsh light on my own exercise of parental forgiveness where my acceptance and approval become bargaining chips offered in exchange for desirable behavior. The gospel is calling me to something far more radical.

It goes without saying that children must be taught responsibility and accountability for their actions, but this cannot come by the withholding of forgiveness or the suggestion that forgiveness requires prior contrition and penance. I am called to examine whether I am willing to let our household share in the paradoxical wisdom of God's household, where it is not a son's inheritance that is wasted prodigally, but the love of the Father. This wastefulness of the love of God keeps coming up in the New Testament faster than I can suppress it. There it is in the parable of the laborers of the vineyard, in which the owner of the vineyard chooses to pay those who only worked a few hours a full day's wage. How dare he? Why waste a full wage when in justice he could pay much less? And then there is the corrupt chief tax-collector, Zacchaeus, climbing a tree to see Jesus but motivated by nothing other than curiosity. Does Jesus confront him with his obvious sins and demand conversion? No, he invites himself in to Zacchaeus's house and lets this radical acceptance do its work. It is the very prodigality of this unconditional acceptance, the sheer wastefulness of the gesture that effects Zacchaeus's conversion. This is how it is in the household of God.

When I say that this practice of forgiveness cannot make contrition and repentance a precondition, this should not be understood as condoning a kind of cheap grace in which nothing is expected of the one being forgiven. To extend forgiveness is to initiate the painful work of restoring relationship. This requires something of both parties. As the one forgiving, I am called to initiate this restoration, but the actual restoration of communion will depend on how that offer is received; without an acknowledgment of wrongs committed and a commitment to address and change the circumstances that effected the rupture of communion, no real restoration of communion is possible. In the parable of the prodigal son, we do not really know how things end. Does the son truly receive the forgiveness of the father and do whatever is necessary on his part to restore communion (e.g., giving himself over to the common labor of the farm, cultivating a sense of gratitude for the father's gracious love)? We do not know. Forgiveness offered is not forgiveness made effective.

Notions of Christian forgiveness have been shaped by our understanding of divine forgiveness. For centuries Christians have spoken of God's forgiveness embodied in the crucifixion of Christ. There is a deep wisdom here, but it has often been distorted because the saving work of the cross was presented variously as paying a ransom (to whom?), forgiving a debt, or absolving from guilt. I believe the crucifixion of Christ as an embodiment of God's forgiveness is best understood as an act of reconciliation, the restoration of communion.[53] St. Paul wrote that in Christ "God was reconciling the world to himself" (2 Cor. 5:19). To forgive is more than paying a ransom or vicariously assuming the punishment of another, it is more than forgiving a debt; it is an attempt to restore or heal relationship.

This is what is demanded of me as a parent, and, for that matter, as a spouse: to embody God's forgiveness by engaging consistently in the kinds of actions that seek to restore and maintain communion with my wife and children. To offer forgiveness in my household is not to engage in a series of magnanimous actions; it is a way of being toward my wife and children. This way of being demands that, in the face of actions that risk breaking our communion with one another, I refuse to accept that brokenness and do whatever I can to restore relationships. It is precisely in my imperfect and halting embodiment of God's forgiveness in all of my actions and attitudes that I am made holy, sanctified, saved.

Embracing Our Children as Gift

The Trinitarian and paschal logic of gift must be cultivated in married life. For married parents our children present us with marvelous opportunities to embrace our lives as gift. My oldest two boys, David and Andrew, are almost eleven years of age now, and I have already begun to recognize some subtle changes. We are an affectionate family, but I have noticed that the older boys are no longer as at ease as they once were with my displaying affection with them in front of their peers. I recently visited them at their school as they were having lunch, and while they were visibly excited to have me sit at the lunchroom table with them, they were less so when I gave them a parting hug. I knew well that what was happening was simply a normal developmental process, yet I felt a sadness that I could not dispel. Two weeks later, the three of us were going to an Astros baseball game when both of them spontaneously grasped my hands on each side as we walked through the parking lot. I acted nonchalantly, holding their hands firmly, while uttering a silent prayer of gratitude, asking only that I be able to treasure the grace of the moment.

Our children's faces are canvases upon which a wondrous

world of emotions and discoveries is painted as if solely for our enjoyment. They laugh and something long dormant stirs within us; they cry and our hearts break. They grow and we discover, as we nurture that growth, the most sublime of vocations. We are blessed in acknowledging their dependence upon us, and blessed again when they grow out of that dependence from children to adolescents and, thanks in no small part to our parental ministrations, become mature, capable, caring adults.

A less obvious gift offered by our children is the way in which they stretch us in such unexpected ways. I derive a tremendous delight from our children, to be sure. Yet I am easily overwhelmed by the emotional demands that parenting makes on me. I tell myself that I would be a great father if I could just submit all of this parenting "stuff" to some kind of reasonable schedule! I keep trying to "manage" this relationship with my kids the way I do with my students. Why can't I establish parenting "office hours"? Yet it is not just the chaos of a noisy household and the emotional demands placed upon me by four growing boys that calls me to the "dying"; it is the children themselves. Whatever Jesus meant when he suggested we must imitate the children, it had nothing to do with angelic innocence! There is no point in hiding it. Our children, who can so often be for us veritable "sacraments" of God's grace, are also imperfect creatures, capable of the same pettiness, resentment, and mean-spiritedness that sets us adults to warring.

I have come to embrace my children as gift in a special way as I discover that it is they who are shaping me every bit as much as I them. Exuberant in play, fierce in anger, yet paradoxically, quick to forgive, I see in my children an emotional clarity that has long since become jumbled and even duplicitous in me. My son Brian has a temper that I keep trying to attribute to his mother's side of the family! When I deny him a request, I am often startled by the emotional force of his anger. Yet ten minutes later he will be sitting on my lap telling me about a school project undertaken with his favorite teacher. From a distance I gaze upon my children and long to know the "cleanness" and purity of their emotions. I lack the confidence in my own emotional life to dare to give it such open and honest expression. And yet there are moments when I shed my status as an emotional bystander and manage to scuffle out of the stands and onto the field of play, wrestling with the boys on the ground, or singing a song with them in the car, that I think, in my communion with them, I may indeed be recapturing some great lost thing.

I wonder if there are people who have brought children into the world who truly have felt that they figured it out, that they mastered the art of parenting. For my part, I feel as if I were on a dinghy cut loose from its moorings and floating wildly down the river. I can make slight course corrections but it is the river that is in charge. I offer those I love most, my wife and children, good intentions, flawed actions, and the commitment to stay the course, even as I hear raging rapids beckoning just around the bend. My married life has much the same feel. I am spouse and parent, husband and father — inseparable vocations. Both call forth from me more than I possess. Both bless me with more than I deserve.

Questions for Reflection and Discussion

1. If you do not have children, what are some other ways in which you have experienced the generative power of your marriage?

2. What are some concrete ways in which your role and responsibilities as a parent have affected your marriage relationship?

3. How has this chapter challenged you to rethink your role as provider, protector, and forgiver?

4. As specifically as you can, try to list all the ways in which you have experienced your spouse and children as gift.

Epilogue

As I write this epilogue our family is in the midst of making a major transition, moving from Houston to Toledo, Ohio. We are leaving not just the state of Texas, the state in which Diana was born and raised, but the state that has, in adulthood, become my adopted home. Almost all of our extended family lives here, as do most of our closest friends. Our twins, David and Andrew, were two months old when we moved to Texas, and it is the only place that Brian and Gregory have ever known. The transition itself is a curious mixture of excitement, sadness, and stress. There is a house to be sold and another to be purchased, furniture to move, ten years of accumulated stuff to sort through and pack, a series of "one-last-time" breakfasts and lunches with friends to be had.

When you live in one place for an extended period of time, marriage and family life take shape within a larger, more comprehensive network of relationships. They blend together, intertwine, often in ways that do not become noticeable until a move is contemplated. Telephones, e-mail, the postal service and cheap airfares guarantee that such transitions need not be as final a break as they were for generations past. Still, when everyone piles into the van and waves goodbye, it hits you in the gut that, within the larger circle of family and friends, some are going and some are not. A family move becomes a stark reminder that however much I have drawn sustenance and support from my extended family and friends, in the end, vows made long ago mean I have cast my lot with this noisy crew. We are bound together, and this bond is both a source of great comfort and a bit unsettling. Any one of us, parent or child, might, if we thought about it, look around and wonder about what might have been, had different choices cast us with a different group of people. But it is idle speculation and we know it. These are our people for good or ill. And so we piled into our two family vehicles: wife, husband, four children, one dog, two hermit crabs, one fish, and a precious croton that has grown with us, immobile and bemused, through our entire marriage.

In Praise of Crotons

I have been thinking about that croton a lot lately. A large plant (or, more accurately, a shrub) noted for its ornamental, leathery leaves, it was one of the items that Diana brought with her into our marriage. Over the years we have thrown out or replaced much of what we each possessed when we were single, old furniture and the like. But the croton has stayed. At one point, when we lived in South Bend, Indiana, a freeze almost killed it as we moved to a new apartment in the dead of winter. It lost all its leaves in a matter of days and we gave it up for dead. Yet weeks later, Lazarus-like, a few tentative sprouts reemerged and it was dubbed our "resurrection plant." Since then it has witnessed any number of dyings and risings within our domicile. It stood tall, without judgment, when Diana and I engaged in many a heated argument, and it blushed not once when our lovemaking healed our wounds and brought forth four boisterous young boys.

The croton stands as a reminder of two tasks or challenges

that marriage presents us, the need for prayer and the call to fidelity. Thomas Merton once wrote: "A tree gives glory to God by being a tree." It is simply by being what they are that trees glorify God. That croton has given glory to God daily in our household, and its quiet immobility reminds us that the most sublime blessings come when we abandon our frantic activity and stand tall and quiet, reflecting back God's glory. It yields no beautiful blossoms to draw attention to itself, and unlike our family pets it neither purrs nor barks nor in any discernible fashion seeks to endear itself to us. Yet it possesses a quiet grace and dignity worthy of emulation. Its very existence is its unceasing prayer to God. With us it is different. We humans give glory to God by becoming the children God has called us to be. We glorify God in our free choices to say yes or no to God's ever present invitation to the life of communion. As such, prayer requires a good deal more effort from us than it does for trees and crotons.

It may seem odd that in a book marketed as an exploration of spirituality there has been so little said about conscious prayer. This should not be interpreted as low regard for the importance of formal prayer. I wrote earlier of the struggles Diana and I have had in learning to pray well *as a couple*. Yet I have found, paradoxically, that as our marriage has proceeded, the hunger for personal prayer has grown. The frenetic pace of our home life has fueled a desperate need to begin each day with a time of solitude in which I set down roots in the love of God. The question of technique continues, and I claim no expertise on this score, but I am convinced that matters of prayer technique are overrated. I have a very dear friend who for the twelve years that I have known him has spent his time in morning prayer silently reading the Gospel of Mark over and over as he paced about the house — without commentary, without journals, without the tools of imaginary prayer often recommended in prayer workshops. He himself would admit that he might easily have chosen another method. What was vital was the sense of a daily grounding in God.

The croton's presence in our lives over these many years teaches us something about fidelity as well. We trumpet the importance of faithfulness in marriage, yet we so quickly reduce it to a negative value — not committing adultery. Fidelity is in a way an eschatological virtue; it is something we aspire to as much as it is something that we experience as a present reality. Fidelity is perhaps the most fundamental challenge we face in our marriage, and none of us is completely up to it. One of the most moving moments in our own married life came when Diana and I participated in a Retrouvaille weekend for couples experiencing difficulties in their marriage. Our twin careers and our children had left us little time for one another. Our marriage was not in threat of dissolution, but it had begun to atrophy, as muscles do from too little exercise.

On the weekend we encountered couples who humbled us with the courage they exemplified as they sought to overcome alcoholism, substance abuse, and multiple affairs. This was no warm, fuzzy retreat; this was, for many of these couples, the last lifeline in a drowning marriage. Fidelity took on new meaning for us that weekend. Fidelity no longer meant simply an unblemished marital record in which one could proudly profess never having cheated on one's spouse. Many of these couples were dealing with adultery. No, fidelity was evoked in the way these couples refused to quit on one another. Fidelity was not something they either possessed or did not; it was something they aspired to, something they clung to as the only thing that separated their broken relationship from the pragmatic romantic arrangements they had experienced prior to their marriage.

Many couples will never experience the horrible damage that an affair can inflict upon a marriage relationship, but no married couple will be exempt from the pain caused by the less significant yet still dangerous exits we make from the demands of our vows. None of us is perfectly faithful; we drift in and out of the attentiveness and charity that our vows demand. Consequently, we can only roughly approximate what God and crotons offer us — perfect, accepting, abiding presence to and for one another. In marriage true fidelity comes to us as hope and task from out of the future of God who is all-faithful.

Marriage and the Domestic Church

One of the great insights of the early church that was re-covered at the Second Vatican Council was the notion that the family constituted by marriage is a kind of church of the home, a domestic church. Certainly for married people, the family is the most basic way in which we experience ourselves drawn into the life of God through our way of being with and for one another. The life of communion celebrated in parishes and dioceses around the world is nurtured as well in the daily give-and-take of married life together. We are, in marriage, a school of discipleship as we seek to become followers of Jesus in the path we have chosen together. Gospel living is incar-nated in actions as simple as choosing to do the laundry at the end of an exhausting day at work, and as great as offering one's home to the homeless. The minutest of marital decisions can give flesh to the Good News of Jesus of Nazareth.

The companionship of marriage calls us to see in our spouses the daily bread Jesus taught us to seek. As companions, husband and wife offer their humble gifts "which earth has given and human hands have made" to church and world that they might be transformed by God's hand. As companions, husband and wife join their eucharistic living with those of others in gathering at the shared feast of the lamb each Sunday.

The community of married life is founded on the most radical of human actions; two people promise themselves, one to another, each casting their lot with this person for the rest of their lives. These promises are most dangerous; they indeed engage us in a daring undertaking. To remain faithful to these promises is to risk everything. It is to walk a tightrope of marital commitment without a net. It means giving up security, comfort, autonomy, control. To marry and to embrace the fruit of marriage is to choose a very particular and demanding way of salvation. To marry is to submit to a crucible of grace. Here the hammer strikes hot iron often as we are being forged into something new, something noble, something of God.

Notes

1. Mary Anne McPherson Oliver, "Conjugal Spirituality (or Radical Proximity): A New Form of Con-templ-ation," *Spirituality Today* 43 (Spring 1991): 54.

2. See Michael G. Lawler, *Marriage and Sacrament: A Theology of Christian Marriage* (Collegeville, Minn.: Liturgical Press, 1993); Theodore Mackin, *What Is Marriage? Marriage in the Catholic Church* (New York: Paulist, 1982).

3. St. Augustine, *Confessions*, Book 1, Chapter 1.

4. Jean Leclercq, "Introduction," in *Bernard of Clairveaux: Selected Works* (New York: Paulist, 1987), 42.

5. The Pastoral Constitution on the Church in the Modern World no. 22. Translation taken from Austin Flannery, ed., *Vatican Council II: Constitutions, Decrees, Declaration* (Northport, N.Y.: Costello, 1996).

6. These modest inferences about Jesus' "hidden years" depend on John P. Meier, *A Marginal Jew: Rethinking the Historical Jesus* (New York: Doubleday, 1991), 1:278–349.

7. References to "brothers and sisters" of one kind or another appear in the following: Mark 3:31–35; 6:3; Matt. 13:55; Acts 12:17; 15:13; 21:18; 1 Cor. 15:7; Gal. 1:19; 2:9, 12; James 1:1; Jude 1.

8. Ronald Rolheiser, *The Holy Longing: The Search for a Christian Spirituality* (New York: Doubleday, 1999), 146.

9. Pierre Teilhard de Chardin, *The Divine Milieu* (New York: Harper & Row, 1969), 65–66.

10. I hasten to add that the evangelical witness of committed celibacy itself is a great gift to the church. I am writing here only of distorted viewpoints.

11. Thomas Merton, *New Seeds of Contemplation* (New York: New Direction Books, 1961), 21.

12. John Zizioulas, *Being as Communion: Studies in Personhood and the Church* (Crestwood, N.Y.: St. Vladimir's Seminary Press, 1985).

13. Michael Downey, *Altogether Gift: A Trinitarian Spirituality* (Maryknoll, N.Y.: Orbis, 2001), 45.

14. Kallistos Ware, "The Sacrament of Love: The Orthodox Understanding of Marriage and Its Breakdown," *Downside Review* (April 1991): 79.

15. Stephen H. Webb, *The Gifting God: A Trinitarian Ethics of Excess* (New York: Oxford University Press, 1996), 93.

16. My reading of this text draws from the analysis of Michael G. Lawler, *Secular Marriage, Christian Sacrament* (Mystic, Conn.: Twenty-Third Publications, 1985), 11–18.

17. Markus Barth, *Ephesians* (New York: Doubleday, 1974), 618.

18. Evelyn Eaton Whitehead and James D. Whitehead, *Marrying Well: Stages on the Journey of Christian Marriage* (Garden City, N.Y.: Doubleday, 1981), 227.

19. Ibid.

20. This felicitous phrase is drawn from the journal of Etty Hillesum, *An Interrupted Life and Letters from Westerbork* (New York: Holt, 1983), 231.

21. Nancy Mairs, *Ordinary Time: Cycles in Marriage, Faith, and Renewal* (Boston: Beacon Press, 1993), 106.

22. Rolheiser, *The Holy Longing: The Search for a Christian Spirituality*, 196.

23. For an extended reflection on this topic see my book, *Transforming Our Days: Spirituality, Community, and Liturgy in a Technological Culture* (New York: Crossroad, 2000).

24. See William Doherty, *Take Back Your Marriage: Sticking Together in a World That Pulls Us Apart* (New York: Guilford Press, 2001).

25. Augustus Napier, *The Fragile Bond: In Search of an Equal, Intimate, and Enduring Marriage* (New York: Harper & Row, 1988).

26. Ibid., 14.

27. Paul Palmer, "Christian Marriage: Contract or Covenant?" *Theological Studies* 33 (1972): 639.

28. Nick Hornby, *High Fidelity* (New York: Riverhead Books, 1995).

29. Ibid., 273.

30. Ibid., 274.

31. Ibid., 241.

32. Ibid., 314–15.

33. Ibid., 318.

34. Rainer Maria Rilke, *Letters to a Young Poet*, rev. ed. (New York: Norton, 1954), 53–54, 57–58.

35. Michael Leunig, *A Common Prayer* (North Blackburn, Australia: Collins Dove, 1990).

36. Karol Wojtyla, *Love and Responsibility* (New York: Farrar, Straus & Giroux, 1981), 270–78.

37. Phyllis Trible, *God and the Rhetoric of Sexuality* (Philadelphia: Fortress Press, 1978), 72–147.
38. Rolheiser, *The Holy Longing: The Search for a Christian Spirituality,* 196.
39. Karen Lebacqz, "Appropriate Vulnerability: A Sexual Ethic for Singles," *Christian Century* 104 (1987): 435–38.
40. Ibid., 437.
41. Luke Timothy Johnson, "A Disembodied 'Theology of the Body,'" *Commonweal* (January 26, 2001): 15.
42. This treatment of *eros* is drawn from Richard Westley, "Marriage, Sexuality and Spirituality," *Chicago Studies* 32 (November 1993): 214–21.
43. *Summa Theologiae* I, q. 98, a. 2. For a comparison of the approaches of Augustine and Aquinas on sexuality see Andre Guindon, *The Sexual Language: An Essay in Moral Theology* (Ottawa: University of Ottawa Press, 1977), 68ff.
44. *Summa Theologiae* II-II, q. 153, a. 2 ad 2.
45. Guindon, *The Sexual Language,* 70.
46. Mitch Finley, "The Dark Side of Natural Family Planning," *America* (February 23, 1991): 207.
47. Oliver, "Conjugal Spirituality," 63–66.
48. Ibid., 63.
49. Vigen Guroian, *Incarnate Love: Essays in Orthodox Ethics* (Notre Dame, Ind.: University of Notre Dame Press, 1987), 31.
50. The crucial sections regarding the morality of artificial birth regulation and the liceity of natural family planning are found in *Humanae vitae,* nos. 14–16.
51. See my book *Transforming Our Days: Spirituality, Community, and Liturgy in a Technological Culture* (New York: Crossroad, 2000).
52. See Finley, "The Dark Side of Natural Family Planning," 206–7.
53. My thoughts on forgiveness have been enriched by L. Gregory Jones, *Embodying Forgiveness: A Theological Analysis* (Grand Rapids, Mich.: Eerdmans, 1995).

Suggested Further Reading

Callahan, Sidney. *Parents Forever: You and Your Adult Children.* New York: Crossroad, 1992.

Doherty, William. *Take Back Your Marriage: Sticking Together in a World That Pulls Us Apart.* New York: Guilford Press, 2001.

Donnelly, Dody. *Radical Love: An Approach to Sexual Spirituality.* Minneapolis: Winston Press, 1984.

Ferder, Fran. *Your Sexual Self: Pathway to Authentic Intimacy.* Notre Dame, Ind.: Ave Maria Press, 1992.

Gallagher, Charles A., et al. *Embodied in Love: Sacramental Spirituality and Sexual Intimacy.* New York: Crossroad, 1984.

Gollwitzer, Helmut. *Song of Love: A Biblical Understanding of Sex.* Philadelphia: Fortress Press, 1979.

Guindon, Andre. *The Sexual Language: An Essay in Moral Theology.* Ottawa: University of Ottawa Press, 1977.

Kasper, Walter. *Theology of Christian Marriage.* New York: Crossroad, 1981.

Lawler, Michael G. *Marriage and Sacrament: A Theology of Christian Marriage.* Collegeville, Minn.: Liturgical Press, 1993.

———. *Secular Marriage, Christian Sacrament.* Mystic, Conn.: Twenty-Third Publications, 1992.

Lebacqz, Karen. "Appropriate Vulnerability: A Sexual Ethic for Singles." *Christian Century* 104 (1987): 435–48.

Mackin, Theodore. *What Is Marriage? Marriage in the Catholic Church.* New York: Paulist, 1982.

Mairs, Nancy. *Ordinary Time: Cycles in Marriage, Faith, and Renewal.* Boston: Beacon Press, 1993.

McDonald, Patrick J., and Claudette M. McDonald. *Can Your Marriage Be a Friendship?* New York: Paulist, 1996.

———. *The Soul of a Marriage.* New York: Paulist, 1995.

Mesa, José M. de. "Marriage as Discipleship." *East Asian Pastoral Review* 28 (1991): 313–96.

Napier, Augustus. *The Fragile Bond: In Search of an Equal, Intimate and Enduring Marriage.* New York: Harper & Row, 1988.

Oliver, Mary Anne McPherson. "Conjugal Spirituality (or Radical Proximity): A New Form of Con-templ-ation." *Spirituality Today* 43 (Spring 1991): 53–67.

Roberts, William P. *Commitment to Partnership: Explorations of the Theology of Marriage.* New York: Paulist, 1987.

Roberts, William P., and Michael G. Lawler, eds. *Christian Marriage and Family: Contemporary Theological and Pastoral Perspectives.* Collegeville, Minn.: Liturgical Press, 1996.

Schillebeeckx, Edward. *Marriage: Secular Reality and Saving Mystery.* New York: Sheed & Ward, 1965.

Tetlow, Elisabeth Meier, and Louis Mulry Tetlow. *Partners in Service: Toward a Biblical Theology of Christian Marriage.* Lanham, Md.: University Press of America, 1983.

Thomas, David M. *Christian Marriage: A Journey Together.* Wilmington, Del.: Glazier, 1983.

Trible, Phyllis. *God and the Rhetoric of Sexuality.* Philadelphia: Fortress Press, 1978.

Westley, Richard. "Marriage, Sexuality and Spirituality." *Chicago Studies* 32 (November 1993): 214–21.

Whitehead, Evelyn Eaton, and James D. Whitehead. *Marrying Well: Stages on the Journey of Christian Marriage.* Garden City, N.Y.: Doubleday, 1981.

Witte, John Jr. *From Sacrament to Contract: Marriage, Religion, and Law in the Western Tradition.* Louisville: Westminster John Knox Press, 1997.

Also by
Richard R. Gaillardetz
Transforming Our Days
Spirituality, Community, and Liturgy
in a Technological Culture
Drawing on his training as a theologian, Gaillardetz explores the subtle
yet pervasive ways in which technology has reshaped our lives. Must
reading for modern couples struggling to raise their
family according to Gospel principles amidst blaring TVs, pop culture,
and the internet.
0-8245-1844-6 $15.95 paperback

Don't Miss these fine books from The Crossroad Publishing Company

Joanne Heany-Hunter and Louis H. Primavera
Unitas
Preparing for Sacramental Marriage
"The Unitas program stands apart from others by cultivating the rela-
tionship between the engaged and the parish community, by its incorpo-
ration of liturgical rites, and by its reliance on theologically sound and
pastorally sensitive presentations."
--Diana Gaillardetz, Pastoral Associate

For more information about this unique marriage preparation program,
please visit our website at www.crossroadpublishing.com.

Leader's Guide
0-8245-1755-5 $19.95 paperback
Couple's Workbook
0-8245-1756-3 $14.95 paperback
Leader's Training Videos (Set of 3)
0-8245-1757-1 $99.00

Pleease support your local bookstore, or call 1-800-707-0670
secure on-line ordering available at:
www.crossroadpublishing.com